So, What Can Kids Do in the Summertime?

Keys to Practical Parenting During School Vacation

Lorraine J. Alldredge

BookWise
publishing

So, What Can Kids Do in the Summertime?
Lorraine J. Alldredge

BookWise Publishing
65 E. Wadsworth Park Drive, Suite 110,
Draper, UT 84020
www.bookwisewritewise.com
801 676-2420

www.bookwiseauthors.com/summertime

Book design: PK Designworks, Highland, Utah

Library of Congress Cataloging-in-Publication Data: Pending

Alldredge, Lorraine J.
So, What Can Kids Do in the Summertime?

ISBN: 978-1-60645-030-7
10 9 8 7 6 5 4 3 2 1
First Printing

PRINTED IN THE UNITED STATES OF AMERICA

Foreword

For most parents, summer vacation can be a bitter-sweet experience. With the kids out of school, the challenge of idleness, too much TV, video games, and mischief—summer can seem interminable and often unbearable. Even vacation trips are a challenge, especially the long hours in the car. Lorraine J. Alldredge, mother of eleven wonderfully normal children, has developed a remarkable program to fill young minds with both purpose and enjoyment while out of school.

As a determined young mother, Lorraine wanted to raise responsible, happy children and the summer months became her opportunity to do so. Mini-classes in cooking, cleaning, and sewing were coupled with group rewards. Her approach to camping and traveling were equally refreshing, boosting those activities from challenges to really fun opportunities. I heartily recommend both the spirit and the transforming details of Lorraine's program to parents everywhere. So, what can your kids do in the summertime? Hopefully, incorporate this book's great activities.

—Richard Paul Evans
#1 *New York Times* bestselling author of *The Christmas Box*

Acknowledgements

I would like to acknowledge the support and cooperation of our eleven children who enthusiastically shared our adventures. During their formative years, we personally implemented nearly every idea presented in this book. They have also been of great help in reviewing the manuscript and in remembering details of our experiences. Most gratifying has been their desire to create similar memories with their own children.

A special recognition goes to our daughter, Kristin Shaeffer, who created all of the illustrations for the book.

I greatly appreciate the help of many of our friends in the book preparation who patiently read the manuscript and offered suggestions and advice. Among them, Brookie and Curt Dickerson were especially helpful and gave us much needed encouragement.

A warm "thank you" goes to the staff of WriteWise, our mentors and agents, for their professionalism, cheerfulness and resourcefulness.

With sincere gratitude, I note the considerable assistance of my loving husband of over forty years, Tony Alldredge. He has been my wise and caring partner in the raising of our family. He was thoroughly supportive of summer goals and of our "traveling with kids" activities and was generally the leader of our camping trips. Although I am listed as the sole author, he has been from the beginning a full partner in the writing of this book.

—Lorraine J. Alldredge

Introduction

I was one of those lucky kids who grew up on a farm. Summertime meant many things, but as a child I had great fun swimming in the ponds and ditches, catching fish in the river, and picking currants from the bushes that grew wild on the ditch banks. These activities filled my summer days with discovery and pleasant memories.

As I grew older, I worked alongside my dad as we cut hay, "combined" the alfalfa seed, or fed the cows. Soon I learned how to do it myself and the responsibility was mine. It was, to me, the perfect way to grow up and spend my summer days. It was also a great way to learn to work hard and take responsibility!

After graduating from high school, I went to college and then married. Since my husband and I wanted a large family, it wasn't long before I found myself the mother of several wonderful children.

Having experienced those summer days of farm work and play, I found it a challenge to keep my growing family busy during the summers in the very different setting of sidewalks and buildings. Most people now live in an urban setting. While this was not undesirable, it presented challenges to this farm girl who wanted to be a good mother. In the city, neighbors were easily accessible, which was wonderful at times but a great distraction at others, especially for a mother who wanted desperately to have her kids near and focused on learning responsibility and having activities of long-lasting value.

Because of those concerns, I devised a plan that helped school vacation take on new meaning. My Summer Goals Program, coupled with other family-centered activities, made this time fun and productive for the entire family. This book is an attempt to share those activities that became a very fulfilling part of our lives, activities that have been copied, with adaptations, by our children.

The traditional family where the father is the sole bread-winner, mom stays at home, generally with more than one child, has become a shrinking minority for many years now. While I believe this type of family provides the best setting for raising children, I recognize that many parents in non-traditional families also love their children dearly and are willing to spend what time and energy they have to teach and care for them.

In *So, What Can Kids Do in the Summertime?*, I leave the deep psychological and sociological analysis to others and explain what has worked for me. I firmly believe that the principles outlined here will help both single parents and working parents if they apply them with determination and love. While personal sacrifice is certainly required, the results will be happier, more responsible children, a healthier society and parents with more joy in their hearts.

—Lorraine J. Alldredge

*To the many children in the world
who yearn daily for the attention and love of their parents.
And to the many parents in this busy world
who yearn daily to know how to give it.*

Table of Contents

So, What Can Kids Do in the Summertime?

Chapter 1

Understanding the Challenge

If you treat a man as he is, he will remain as he is,
but if you treat him as if he were what he ought to be, and could be,
he will become what he ought to be, and should be.
—Goethe

School Vacation and Mixed Feelings

Have you ever found yourself thinking about school vacation with mixed emotions? You dream of shared activities and help with the chores, but often find yourself dealing with too much TV, video games and bickering. If you're a working parent, you worry about the kids at home alone with nothing to do. What are you going to do to fill those summer days? How can you possibly keep the kids from too many long hours of idleness or unsupervised play with their friends? School vacation should include time to relax, explore, and develop friendships, but without a bit of structure, kids can become bored and develop a pattern of idleness, indulgence and mischief.

A Time for Strengthening Family Ties

During the school year, a great deal of a child's attention is focused on academics, sports and relationships outside the home. School vacation is a parent's opportunity to focus on family relationships and to teach the skills that children will need as they become adults to be able to care for themselves and their families. In addition, this is often the only block of time available for major family activities such as camping and traveling. In Chapters 7 and 8, you will discover how to better enjoy these activities and use them to strengthen family ties.

There is a temptation to rely on summer camps to fill the void left by school activities. A good summer camp might keep kids occupied for a time, but it will not bring you closer together, nor will it teach your kids the things they need to learn about home and family.

Family relationships have a deep and enduring influence. After studying the rise in juvenile delinquency from 1991 to 1999, Dr. Karol L. Kumpfer wrote for the US Department of Justice that ". . . improving parenting practices and the family environment is the most effective and enduring strategy for reducing juvenile delinquency and associated behavioral and emotional problems . . . We believe that strengthening the ability of families to raise children to be law-abiding and productive citizens should be one of the most critical public policy and social issues in the United States." (Kumpfer, 1999)

The kids' time away from school should be used, not wasted. This time, whether during the summer or scattered throughout the year, seems like a few short weeks, but if you add those days together, *school vacation is equivalent to nearly three years —three important, formative years.* That valuable time should not be devoted too much to entertainment, especially given the urgency of teaching kids how to succeed in a family.

The TV — Getting Control

One of the first challenges is to get your kids' attention. Children in the US watch a great deal of television, even during the school year. Additional hours are spent with video games and on computers. Even more time is typically spent on these activities during school vacation. TV and other electronic media can be helpful tools or terrible masters. Several prestigious institutions and researchers have recently noted that excessive television watching can weaken childrens' power of imagination, give them a confused view of real life, lead to apathetic or overactive behavior, and interfere with true learning. (Anderson and Wilkins, 1998, pp. 38-39)

When our children were young, we experienced times when our TV was broken. We purposefully took several months to repair or buy another, and after each time, we set more firm limits on its use. During the school year, television was generally off-limits on school nights, which allowed time for homework and music practice without the distraction of a TV program blaring in the background. During school vacation, TV time was limited to a few hours each day. These restrictions have been a great blessing to our entire family.

If you want to control TV watching, I recommend that you first make notes on what you watch and analyze what you have found. Discuss as a family how TV can be good and how it can hurt, paying particular attention to its effects on the youngest children. Next, set a period of abstinence, perhaps a week or two. This allows the entire family to demonstrate control over the media and to re-discover other activities. Then write down your own rules for a selective, intelligent viewing schedule and check periodically to assure that you are sticking to those rules.

The same approach will help you control video game use. Anderson and Wilkins (1998) outlines a similar approach in more detail and give keys to success. For the full reference, see the Additional Resources section near the end of this book. If you are firm in setting and maintaining reasonable rules, your entire family will gain more from your use of electronic media and you will be more able to control those activities when it is time for your Summer Goals Program and family summer activities.

A Flexible Program

The activities described in this book can be easily adapted to long or short school vacations, year-round school, weekends or evenings. They work with large families and small. The key is to use the basic ideas to design a program that is wholesome for the kids in your home and to work on it together. Some parents can be at home during school vacation while others must work. Do what you can. These activities will help you use your available time to strengthen your family and teach your kids the skills that build the character traits they will need to eventually care for their own family.

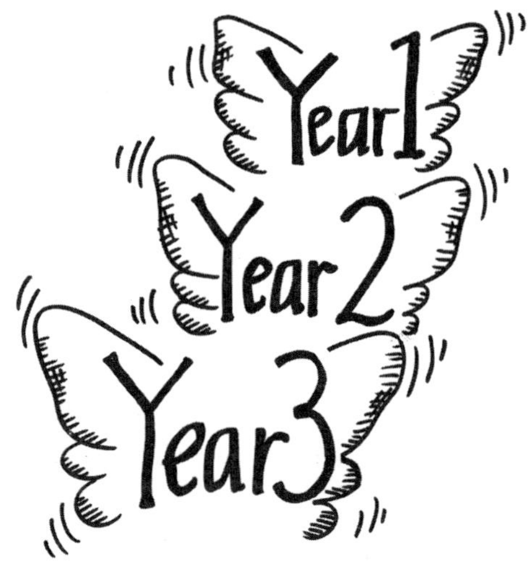

Summer vacation is equivalent to three important years— one quarter of a child's life during their school years.

Chapter 2
Setting Summer Goals and Rewards

*"Home ought to be our clearinghouse,
the place from which we go forth lessoned and disciplined,
and ready for life."*
—Kathleen Norris

Summer Goals - Getting Started

As a mother, I felt that school vacation was valuable time with my kids and I did not want to give too much of it up to TV, programs outside the home, or neighbors. My husband and I both wanted our kids to learn to work, to be responsible, and to learn to set goals and reach them. Why not incorporate these principles into a program and make this a season for fun and learning combined? And so the idea of the summer goals program was born. Our purpose was to have the kids work toward meaningful objectives and celebrate their accomplishment with a reward. The program involved four fundamental steps which I followed as we approached each school vacation. If your school scatters its vacation time throughout the year, you will want to re-define your program at the end of each school year or session.

After careful reflection, I found it was most effective for me to decide what I wanted each of my kids to accomplish and simply tell them what their goals should be. You may choose to have your kids be more involved in setting their own individual goals, but I recommend you first go through these steps by yourself and determine what is negotiable and what is not.

1st — I carefully considered each of my kids, their ages and their abilities. I did not want to underestimate their potential for learning, nor did I want to set them up for failure.

2nd — I made a list of fundamental "life management" skills I wanted my kids to learn, such as:

- cleaning
- cooking
- sewing
- writing
- reading
- memorizing
- music
- quilting

The possibilities for skill development are endless. Your list may include seventy-seven items or just two. Here are some other ideas of skills you may want to tackle: drawing or painting, washing and ironing, learning words of a foreign language, maintaining personal hygiene, growing a garden, mowing the lawn, washing the car, woodworking (for an older child), or changing a tire (also for an older child).

Money management is certainly a fundamental life management skill and you may choose to include it in your summer goals. Our older kids have benefited from carefully writing down all their income and expenses for several months, helping them see where their money is going. However, we chose to address this issue separately from summer goals – see A Note About Allowances and Daily Chores later in this book.

On a farm, the work is often different. However, in a city household, we assigned tasks that accomplished the same end results. Boys and girls both needed to learn responsibility and to be busy. Mowing the lawn seemed to us a job more for the boys, but the girls often took their turn. It certainly doesn't hurt a boy to wash the dishes, mop the floor, clean the bathroom or organize drawers and cupboards. In today's world where husband and wife often both work outside the home, everyone needs to know how to help with all the chores and tasks.

3rd — I set goals for each child suited to that child's potential and personality. In each area of interest, I listed how many times a task should be formally signed-off during the summer, both to assure that the child learned the skill and to help with the housework. That first year our kids ranged in ages from one to twelve and, of course, I had different expectations for different ages. The younger ones needed considerable help while the older ones were expected to learn more quickly and to perform the work more frequently.

4th — I selected an appropriate group activity to celebrate success. It is much more motivating to work toward a goal when you have a tangible reward in sight.

Mini-Classes and Sign-Off Sheets

I decided that successful mastery of a skill would require a certain level of perfection. Daily chores would be acceptable, at least temporarily, at a slightly lower standard, so I kept those duties separate from the Summer Goals Program. For the kids to attain the higher standard that I wanted, I needed to show them what was expected in brief mini-classes. A mini-class can be a quick explanation or a thirty-minute demonstration, depending on the needs and attention span of the child and on the time you have available. A short explanation is better than none. Some skills, such as cleaning or cooking, require quite a bit of training and supervision, while others, such as reading or writing, require very little.

The kids understood the cleaning process better if it was written down, step by step, on a card and taped inside a cupboard or closet in the room involved. When the child was ready for me to approve their mastery of a skill, I inspected their work. If the task was completed to my satisfaction, I initialed their goal sheet. The younger children preferred to see a sticker or gold star at completion.

Requiring my kids to master the skill gave me hope that they would remember it when they grew into adulthood, and I required them to pass off some skills more than once. I was careful to mark the completion of a goal and to offer a warm "well done." This is very important since kids note the way you follow through with what you say. If you don't provide recognition and encouragement, the kids will lose enthusiasm for the program. Every year builds on the prior one and you will want your kids to carry a positive outlook into each new school vacation.

Rewards

As each of my kids completed their summer goals they were pleased with themselves and looked forward to celebrating. Because we did not eat out much, the reward for reaching summer goals that first summer was a family trip to *Wendy's* for dinner. That may not seem like a big treat now, but at the time it was for us. We made "I did it!" buttons for everyone to wear. That was a bit cheesy, looking back, but we all felt that we had worked hard for that day. The kids were pleased because they had accomplished a list of goals and I was pleased because as a family it had been a very productive summer.

As the years went by, our celebrations grew and included a day long visit to the city's water park, an afternoon at a skating rink, and a day bicycling several miles through a city park. Each outing was carefully planned and included special treats and activities.

I preferred to celebrate as a family rather than individually. This encouraged the kids to help each other if one was lagging. To show flexibility, I allowed the kids to participate in the event if all but one goal was completed. There still were occasions when a child was excluded because they did not complete enough of their goals. While this is not easy and can usually be avoided with extra encouragement and planning, the reward is not really a reward if it cannot be lost. Kids need to learn to handle consequences, a lesson taught harshly by the world if not learned in the home.

One of our daughters, now the mother of six, prefers individual rewards so they can be personalized. One year each of her kids had a one-on-one "date" with Mom or Dad where each chose a reasonable destination. An individual approach allows parents to celebrate sooner for the early finishers and allows the slower kids more time. The slower ones are motivated to finish when they see their siblings celebrating their success. Personalized celebrations will work best for some families while group rewards are better for others. Assess your situation and do what you think is best for your kids.

While having a tangible reward is important, especially to younger children, remember that the most important results are by-products. Besides the skills learned, the summer goal process also teaches kids how to work with those in authority, how to complete a personal objective, appreciation for the results of work, patience, and many other life management skills. It also helps parents and children to better understand one another and draws them closer together.

The reward of a thing well done, is to have done it.
—Ralph Waldo Emerson

Clues to Success

As you establish summer goals for your own kids, the following concepts will be helpful:

- Set proper expectations before the summer starts. If a child expects complete freedom, summer goals will seem confining. Let the kids know a month or so ahead of time that you have a summer program for them that includes meaningful goals and rewards. Then a week or two before the start of school vacation give them their detailed goals and discuss them one-on-one.

- The pace of goals should be enough to challenge, but not enough to discourage the child. Keep kids busy doing good, positive and practical activities and they won't be as likely to get into trouble. But remember that this program is to benefit the child, not the parents. Tailor the goals to the child. Be patient; they will do more the next year. Make the program reasonable so they can enjoy growing in the activity. Set enough goals so the child does not finish too early in the summer. Encourage each child to pass off a goal every day or two so they do not leave too many for the end of the summer.

- Keep summer goals separate from daily chores such as making their bed, putting toys away, emptying the trash, etc. Everyone should help with regular housekeeping as part of their membership in the family and these duties continue throughout the year. Summer goals require more time and attention and have a definite completion date with a special reward. If the two were combined, both regular chores and the goals program would become bogged down with too much tracking and detail.

- Do not be afraid to start young. Children are more enthused at age three or four and this is not too young if you start simply. It helps to set a pattern of learning while the child is young. Start with the basics and allow the child's ability to grow each summer. Starting young and being patient may take a bit more effort for the parent, but it pays off in the end.

- As your older kids begin to find employment outside the home, you will want to cut back on their goals because they have less time. You will still find that these activities bring you together, even if your child only has to bake bread a couple of times during the summer, sew one article of clothing, read a book or two, or learn a few new songs. Setting an objective, working together to achieve it and then sharing the reward is a positive experience at any age.

- Consider setting a goal or two for yourself. As you fulfill meaningful objectives, you set an example for your kids. Your participation in a group reward then has added meaning.

Sample Sheets

I have included samples of my summer goals sheets, but feel free to draft your own. A blank sheet is included in Appendix A, along with more examples. You may choose, as I did, to make a standard list of basic goals, changing each year the number of times it is to be completed and adding a few new goals appropriate for each child. If a child is too young to complete that task alone, you may assist the child or that line may be left blank.

We kept the lists of summer goals in a readily accessible place—inside the coat closet off the dining room. One of our daughters who is setting summer goals in her own home now posts them next to the light switch in the kids' bedrooms.

Summer Goals for <u>Girl Age 15</u>

How Many Times	Item	Completed
4	Clean drawers (her own)	
2	Clean drawers (family)	
6	Wash and dry laundry (family)	
3	Clean windows	
Help	Make a quilt	
2 blouses & skirt	Sew article of clothing	
4	Clean bathroom	
1	Clean closet (her own)	
1	Clean closet (family)	
2	Clean cupboard (family)	
4	Vacuum the floor	
2	Clean car	
1	Bake cookies from scratch	
1	Bake cake from scratch	
1	Bake sweet rolls from scratch	
1	Bake dinner rolls from scratch	
3	Bake bread from scratch	
2	Make dinner (family)	
2	Make breakfast (family)	
20 pages	Write in journal	
5	Learn new piece on piano	
1	Learn new piece on violin	
1	Learn new vocal solo	

Summer Goals for __Boy Age 9__

How Many Times	Item	Completed
2	Clean drawers (his own)	
2	Clean drawers (family)	
2	Wash and dry laundry	
2	Clean windows	
Help	Make a quilt (family)	
1	Sew article of clothing	
2	Clean bathroom	
1	Clean closet (his own)	
1	Clean closet (family)	
2	Clean cupboard (family)	
4	Vacuum the floor	
2	Clean car	
Help	Bake cookies from scratch	
Help	Bake cake from scratch	
Help	Bake sweet rolls from scratch	
Help	Bake dinner rolls from scratch	
Help	Bake bread from scratch	
Help 1 & 1 alone	Make dinner (family)	
2	Make breakfast (family)	
1 page	Journal	
3	Learn new vocal piece	
2	Learn new piano piece	
50 to 100	Read children's books	
Once a week	Study math facts	

A Note for Working Parents

When both parents work, summer is an even greater challenge. I believe that no one can provide the training and nurturing that a family can. I know many parents have to work to provide necessities and I know also that parents themselves have needs. But no matter what the parental situation is, you must consider the needs of the children.

The Summer Goals Program provides a practical, home-based plan for the summer, most of which can be completed by the kids in the parents' absence. Mom or Dad can work out the goals and give the mini-classes on a day when they don't work outside the home. A lunch time phone call from the office can provide a status report and a reminder. Most kids respond well to purposeful rules and structure, especially if the pattern is set while they are young. This program clarifies the goals that are expected, how to fulfill them, and what the rewards will be. Kids work on their own schedule with time for socializing and for play.

The Summer Goals Program will not fully occupy your kids' vacation days and will not remove the need for adult supervision, but it will add purpose and structure and help draw your family together. A nanny or baby sitter will be greatly assisted by a plan of responsibilities and activities for the kids in their care.

Be patient but firm on the basics: 1) school vacation is an important time for the family to learn and enjoy something together; 2) certain life skills are fundamental to happy home life (see the second step of the goals program); 3) work together to complete meaningful goals during school vacation; and 4) everyone may enjoy a reward at the completion of their goals. Find what works for your family. Even a modest, consistent effort on your part can bring great benefits in the long run to both you and your kids.

Experiment with different approaches. Every hour spent working, learning or playing with your child builds your relationship with them and teaches by your example. Ask the kids what will work for them, especially if your kids are older or are strong-willed. Try having the kids report on their accomplishments at the end of the day. Set both individual and group rewards at the same time—individual rewards to recognize individual effort and a group reward to be enjoyed only if all complete their goals. The group celebration should, hopefully, inspire the kids to encourage each other.

Dinners can be part of the goals with older kids helping younger ones. Wouldn't it be wonderful to occasionally come home to a dinner prepared by the kids? A beginning goal might be for the kids to set the table. They can then progress to prepare a single dish such as a salad, boiled vegetables or a sheet cake. Later they can be taught to cook a simple dinner (see the recipes in Chapter 4). If this is approached with a positive attitude it will not become a heavy burden. Give them a cookbook and let them choose a dish for you to teach to them on a day off work, then set a day for them to prepare the same dish by themselves. Praise whatever they do and gently coach them through needed improvements.

If an older child is supervising younger siblings, be sure to make their reward or celebration extra special. Include frequent one-on-one time with that child at least weekly to emphasize your appreciation and to address problems they may be dealing with. Remember that this child will have nearly adult responsibility. Be sure they have adult help available in an emergency.

Testimonials

One of our daughters, referring to summer goals set with her own kids, reports: "I've found that most children respond well to lists that can be checked off as each task or goal is accomplished. One of my children is a particularly good example. He loves the 'black and white' routine of the day. He can focus on each assignment easily and gets a kick out of checking it off. Then, with no questions or worry of boredom, he is on to the next task. Another of my children seems oblivious to the whir of productivity around him. He wonders where the time goes. The other children will be checking things off, while he is still thinking about it. This child's heart is in the right place, he just clicks differently. To help him, we determine what task he will work on and I set a buzzer. He needs more attention and follow-up, but I have given him this aid so that he is not constantly discouraged. He has missed out on our celebration outing before because I don't do his summer goals for him."

Another daughter, now grown, says that whenever she was bored she would go to the coat closet and review her summer goals. At a glance she could see several ideas for things to do and would be instantly reminded of goals she was working toward. She remembers deep 'spring cleaning' types of chores, ambitious baking projects, journal writing, quilt-making, and learning extra piano pieces. She also remembers formal mini-classes that I conducted in order to teach her a new recipe or cleaning procedure and she remembers other times when only brief instructions were needed. She says, "Looking back, I realize the invaluable experience it gave me. I learned and developed much-needed skills, but more importantly, I developed a desire to be industrious, to contribute to a greater whole, and to enjoy accomplishing my goals."

In setting goals with her own kids she notes, "I admit it sometimes turns out to be a list of things I will be required to 'help' do each summer. Still, it is an effective plan of action, and frankly, I need such a list! As my children get older, there are more and more items on the list that they can accomplish independently. In the meantime, it keeps me on a proactive track. And summers are MUCH more fun for all of us!"

A third daughter, the mother of four boys, ages eight to fourteen, contributes the following: "When most families were raised in an agricultural environment, boys often had very clear-cut responsibilities and plenty of opportunities to learn to work. These are the things that kept them busy and out of trouble. Their work opportunities taught them the value of hard work and molded their character as men. Now, most boys are raised in an urban or suburban setting and often the most required of them is mowing the lawn. Oft times not even this duty is delegated to them. Consequently, there is little to keep them busy other than sports and 'hanging out' with friends—hardly activities that will develop men of priority and goal-setting or prepare a young man for a lifetime in the workplace. While sports, schoolwork and friends can play an important role in the development of young men, parents need to get creative when it comes to teaching young men and boys how to work in a suburban setting. For me, this means that the strict gender roles of yesteryear may need to be modified.

"I have utilized the Summer Goals Program since my boys were very young, adjusting goals through the years to reflect age-appropriate goals and objectives. They know now how to make reasonably good bread, fix dinner, clean their closets and do the laundry. Whenever possible, we provide our boys with opportunities for 'manly' goals, such as planting, tending, or weeding the garden, mowing lawns, etc., but I feel strongly that we should not shield our boys from the duties readily available in an urban setting. I feel grateful for this program because I know that it has helped my four boys appreciate work in all its varieties and taught them how to set goals and feel the satisfaction of achieving them."

Yet another daughter says, "My family and I have loved setting summer goals! There are so many benefits! It establishes a time line for issues you might otherwise allow to stretch on and on. The program provides our children with something constructive to do in the summer that gives them a deep sense of accomplishment. It is a vehicle to accomplish random jobs that I might rarely get to and it gives me an opportunity to teach the kids how to do certain things without coming across as pushy. Most satisfying for us, as parents, is sharing a reward with the kids that they have earned (circus, horseback riding, water or theme park, etc.). We will certainly continue with summer goals!"

My oldest son, not yet married, adds, "I believe that my natural tendency to establish and work toward specific goals was enhanced by the Summer Goals Program. I am deeply grateful to my parents for that exercise because it has led me to identify my dreams and work to realize them. I remember the satisfaction of completing the goals even more than the rewards. Physical rewards are important, of course, especially for young children, but at some point completion of the task becomes its own reward. The most valuable reward was the pattern of working toward a goal, then relaxing and evaluating your performance. I also appreciate the intent of the goals which was to teach us to clean, cook and read for ourselves. It has led us all to be more organized, well-rounded and self-reliant."

The Summer Goals Program can change the atmosphere in your home. It can change a summer of boredom and bickering into a summer of fun and learning. It had a profound impact on our kids and on our home. Try it and see for yourself.

Chapter 3
Cleaning Skills

Cleanliness is next to Godliness.

—Ancient Proverb

Cleaning Cards

Cleaning skills are perhaps the most basic of all household skills. Everyone enjoys a clean house and life in such a home is more healthy and productive. As with most things, moderation is important. It is better to have kids committed to moderate cleaning than to push too hard and have them dislike cleaning so much they refuse to do it later. It also helps to remember that a home is a place for the family to live in, not just a showplace for visitors.

To some, the topic of cleaning is a distasteful one. However, the very real alternatives are chaos and poor health. This should be carefully explained to kids and modeled by mom and dad. Learning how to clean is a maturing experience and should not be dodged.

It helps to set clear expectations by writing down the cleaning steps, perhaps on an index card. Posting the card in an easily accessible place keeps it readily available for reference. The work list for cleaning the living room might look like this:

Cleaning the Living Room

1. Pick up items that do not belong in the room and put them away.
2. Dust all furniture.
3. Dust windowsills and baseboards.
4. Clean any mirrors with glass cleaner and a clean rag or paper towel.
5. Shake any rugs outside.
6. Put the rugs back in their proper place after vacuuming the floor.
7. Vacuum the entire floor at least twice.

The card for cleaning the bathroom might look like the card below. Tape the card inside the bathroom cupboard so the kids can reference it easily.

Cleaning the Bathroom

1. Clean the sink and counter with cleaner.
2. Clean the toilet bowl, seat, tank and outside bowl with cleaner.
3. Clean the tub or shower with cleanser or tile cleaner.
4. Shine all chrome faucets and handles with clean cloth or a paper towel.
5. Clean the mirror with window spray and shine it with a clean cloth or paper towel.
6. Shake the rugs.
7. Take out the trash.
8. Sweep and mop the floor.
9. Put the rugs and trash baskets back in place.

A Note about Allowances and Daily Chores

A note or two about allowances and daily chores may be helpful. We have always kept these issues separate from summer goals and their rewards. Finances and basic housekeeping continue all during the year and have purposes that are different from summer goals. There are, of course, many ways to handle allowances and chores. Your approach will work if you are clear, consistent and fair with your kids. As with summer goals, these issues provide many excellent teaching moments for young minds and hearts.

Just as I was not paid for my duties when I was young, we did not pay our kids for small assignments that were everyone's responsibility. So the young children could learn to manage money, we gave a modest allowance to each of the kids until they were old enough to earn money outside the home. This allowance was not tied to completion of their daily chores because we did not want the kids to feel they had to be paid for doing their share of maintaining the home. For these same reasons, I do not recommend money as a reward for completion of summer goals.

Ideas to Add Spice to Daily Chores

- Rotate assignments. This can be done with a 'job wheel' or other innovative chore chart. You can rotate chores weekly, monthly or whatever works best for you. Change itself is restful and reduces boredom.

- Try an occasional deviation from routine assignments by writing all assignments on slips of paper and put them folded in a bowl. Kids pull a job from the bowl. When that job is completed, they return for another until all of the jobs are completed.

- Have a 'chore treasure hunt.' When I did it, this was loads of fun, especially for younger children, but required more of my time to prepare, so I did not do it often. I prepared an individual 'treasure hunt' for each child with directions to clues around the house that designated jobs to be done. At the start of the 'hunt' I directed each of the kids to the location of their first clue, perhaps under a pillow or in a drawer. At that location they found a note explaining the job to be performed and telling them where to find the next clue after that job was completed. After several successive clues and assignments, they were directed to a final location where they found a 'treasure,' perhaps a sack lunch under a tree.

- Establish a 'job jar.' During the week, one of our daughters, as she notices special jobs that need to be done, writes them on a slip of paper and puts them in a jar. Then as time allows or when a child requests it, she has them pull an assignment from the jar. When the assignment is completed she gives them a treat.

- Gather all the kids together and decide on a room in which to begin cleaning the house. Set the buzzer for a challenging completion time. Then work together as a team to clean each of the rooms in turn, trying to beat the buzzer.

- Play a favorite music CD or tune to a preferred radio station while cleaning. A friend of ours has a favorite song with an upbeat rhythm that she plays while cleaning.

Chapter 4
Cooking Skills

A child becomes an adult when he realizes
that he has a right not only to be right but also to be wrong.
—Thomas Szasz

The Basics

In many families, home cooking has given way to eating out, pre-cooked meals and fast food. Having meals together is also losing its priority, despite dinner time being a prime time for visiting and strengthening family ties. Cooking at home can save money, sixty percent or more in my experience, and can be healthier than eating out, especially when compared to fast food.

In May 2008 the *Pensacola News Journal* wrote, quoting Rachel Brandeis of the American Dietetic Association, "People consume 50% more calories, fat and sodium when they eat out than when they cook at home." (Suchcicki, 2008)

The summer goals program is a great way to introduce your kids to home cooking. One of our daughters especially liked completing summer goals for cooking and baking and even helped support herself in college by selling her home-baked bread.

Teaching kids to cook takes just a bit of patience and generosity. Most basic food is not expensive and the kids need to develop confidence, so let them make a mess occasionally or spoil a few dishes of food. They need to gain experience and enjoy the interaction with Mom or Dad. Often when I was preparing dinner I had a couple of chairs pushed up to the counter with little kids helping. It certainly would have been easier without that "help," but it was well worth it—my kids are great cooks now and we had a wonderful time getting there.

Some kitchen equipment can cause harm if not used carefully, so teach safety rules for the stove, toaster, mixer and knives before beginning. Very young children certainly should not be using a steak knife or the stove, but they can roll out cookies and spread jam or butter with a spoon. Begin teaching children when very young that the stove will burn, that they should never pull on the handle of a pan on the stove (or it will spill hot food on them), that only older ones turn on the mixer or use a knife, etc. Soon, little ones can be trusted with a butter knife and can learn to cut butter, cheese, soft vegetables and fruit, and bread. With a bit of coaching, older kids can learn to safely use the stove and other kitchen equipment.

When it comes to summer goals, start with easy things. Master one skill at a time before adding to it. You might want to begin by teaching young children to make a basic sandwich or graham cracker cookies with powdered sugar frosting. They might then learn to use the microwave oven to warm leftovers, to heat packaged soup or vegetables or to pop popcorn. As soon as they can use the equipment safely, they can learn how to make soup from a can, scramble an egg, peel an orange or make a milks hake in the blender.

Below are recipes for a few items that you can teach kids to prepare. French toast is an easy breakfast to start with. You can then move on to pancakes. Cookies are among the easiest items to bake and are always in demand. Later you can try baking fresh bread— it is not that hard to do and it adds to any meal. It also makes the house smell great! When your kids are ready to move on to dinners, shepherd's pie and Chinese fried rice are easy dinners to prepare and have almost everything in one dish.

There are cookbooks of all kinds available with recipes for salads, soups, main dishes and desserts to round out your cooking skills.

Recipes

If you are looking for some easy recipes to start with, you will like these.

Applesauce Cookies

½ cup shortening

2 eggs

1 level teaspoon
baking soda

½ level teaspoon cinnamon

½ level teaspoon cloves

½ level teaspoon nutmeg

½ level teaspoon salt

1 cup sugar

1 cup applesauce

2 cups flour (I like whole wheat flour, but some prefer white)

1 cup nuts (optional)

1 package (7 oz) chocolate chips or raisins (optional)

Mix applesauce and soda together. Mix sugar, shortening and eggs in a separate bowl. Combine applesauce and shortening mix. Sift flour and spices into wet ingredients. Add nuts and chocolate chips. Drop by spoonfuls onto a greased and floured cookie sheet. Bake 10 minutes at 375 degrees.

You can make pumpkin cookies from this recipe by substituting canned pumpkin for applesauce and adding 1 level teaspoon ginger.

French Toast

1 Egg

¼ cup milk

Sliced bread

A pinch of sale and a pinch of cinnamon or nutmeg (this last is
   optional)

Mix all ingredients in a mixing bowl. Dip both sides of each slice of bread in the mix. Place dipped bread slices in a hot, greased frying pan until brown. Turn over and brown the other side. Serve with butter and maple syrup. Serves one. Multiply ingredients to serve your family.

Pancakes

1 cup flour

1 cup milk

1 egg

2 Tablespoons oil

1 level Tablespoon sugar

2 level teaspoons baking powder

¼ level teaspoon salt

Put wet ingredients in a bowl and mix. Sift dry ingredients into the wet ingredients and mix enough to blend ingredients, but do not beat. Pancakes are more fluffy if mixed lightly. Spoon into a hot, greased frying pan until bubbles start to pop, then turn once. Serve with butter and maple syrup. Makes about six medium-sized pancakes. Multiply ingredients to serve the family.

Bread

>   5 cups warm water
>
>   6 level Tablespoons shortening
>
>   6 level Tablespoons sugar
>
>   2 level Tablespoons salt
>
>   3 yeast cakes or 3 level Tablespoons dry yeast
>
>   About 10 to 12 cups flour

Dissolve yeast and sugar in about one cup of the warm water in a large mixing bowl. Add all other ingredients except flour, then add enough flour to make a medium-stiff dough. Knead about 5 minutes, either by hand or in mixer. Put in a covered bowl. I have found that the raising process speeds up if you do the following: after 5 minutes, punch down; after 5 more minutes, punch down; after 15 minutes, punch down; wait 30 minutes, then form into loaves and let rise about 35 to 60 minutes (until double in bulk). Bake for 35 to 45 minutes at about 350 degrees. This recipe makes four large loaves or 5 medium loaves.

Chinese Fried Rice

4 cups cooked and cooled white rice (to cook the rice follow the instructions on the box)

3 to 5 green onions, chopped

1 can Spam or 1 cup ham, diced

2 Tablespoons Soy Sauce

4 eggs

Heat and brown rice in a greased frying pan. Stir in onions; add ham; add soy sauce; add eggs and cook until eggs are done. Optional: add frozen green peas or mixed vegetables.

Shepherd's Pie

1 lb. ground beef

1 medium onion

3/4 level teaspoon salt

Dash of black pepper

Two 1 lb. cans of green beans

One 10 oz. can tomato or cream of mushroom soup

5 medium potatoes, boiled

1/2 cup milk

1/4 cup butter (optional)

Lightly brown meat in a frying pan. Add the onion and cook until tender. Mix seasonings, beans and soup into meat mix. Pour into a 1 1/2 quart casserole dish. Mash potatoes and add milk and butter. Season potatoes lightly with salt and pepper and drop into mounds over the meat and bean mix. If desired, sprinkle with 1/2 cup shredded cheddar cheese. Bake at 350 degrees for 25 to 30 minutes.

Chapter 5
Other Valuable Skills

If a teacher influences but one, his influence never stops.
—Greek

Reading

Reading books is a great summer goal and can help kids transition back into school. "Staying in training as a learner over the longer summer break between school years is critical so that students hold on to prior learning and return to school in September with the behaviors and attitudes for new learning to take hold." (NYU, 2004) "Children who continue to read during the summer months 'exercise their brains,' which is great preparation for when school resumes in the fall. By reading, your child will actually build his or her language and thinking skills. One key to a child's reading success is making the reading experience entertaining, relaxing and enjoyable. Allow your child to choose his or her own reading materials." (NYU, 2006)

The following magazines have articles that appeal to young readers:

- Highlights for Children
- American Girl
- Disney
- Disney Princess
- Backyard Adventures
- Boys Life

Our town library had a great summer reading program with awards for meeting established requirements and that program was an important part of our summer goals. See what your local library offers and assist your kids in obtaining their own library cards. Older kids might have a goal to provide a brief book report to the family, also sharpening their writing or oral presentation skills. Younger children love to read to their parents. When parents listen to their child read, the child feels important and the parents can evaluate the child's progress as a reader.

If your children are too young to read by themselves, they will enjoy having you read to them. Bedtime is an excellent time to read to your children, because it calms them down so they can fall asleep. Listening to more advanced stories also stimulates their imagination and encourages them to read. Some of our favorite bedtime stories were *Little House on the Prairie, The Hobbit, Anne of Green Gables, Hardy Boys, Nancy Drew* and *The Little Princess.* Some of our friends have recommended *The Indian in the Cupboard and Chronicles of Narnia.* The *Read-Aloud Handbook* by Jim Trelease (Penguin Books, 1982) also has excellent recommendations for reading to your children.

> *You may have tangible wealth untold;*
> *Caskets of jewels and coffers of gold.*
> *Richer than I you can never be—*
> *I had a Mother who read to me.*

—"The Reading Mother" by Strickland Gillilan
from *Best Loved Poems of the American People*

Stories often raise questions that prompt good discussions. Don't be afraid to address questions of morality, justice, religion, how to deal with fear, etc. The children really want to know what you believe and will be forming their own ideas soon. If you don't have a good answer, saying "I don't know" or "I'm not sure" teaches them to be honest and to work through difficult questions. Your honest answers will give more comfort and direction than you might expect.

Simple stories are best for very young children, but by the age of five or six they often like a more involved tale. A story that frightens younger children might be good for those of nine or ten. The following is a short list of books that kids in the early grades might be ready to read:

Amelia Bedelia series by Peggy Parish

Boxcar Children series by Gertrude Chandler Warner

Charlotte's Web by E. B. White

The Emperor's New Clothes by Hans C. Andersen

The Hare and the Tortoise by Aesop

The Steadfast Tin Soldier by Hans C. Andersen

The Velveteen Rabbit by Margery Williams

The World of Christopher Robin by A. A. Milne

The following books might be good reading for kids nearing sixth or seventh grade, or for you to read to kids of any age:

Abe Lincoln Grows Up by Carl Sandburg

Abraham Lincoln or Benjamin Franklin or others in the series
 by I. and E. D'Aulaire

Alice's Adventures in Wonderland by Lewis Carroll

American Revolution by Richard Morris

Anne of Green Gables series by L. M. Montgomery

Arabian Nights by Andrew Lang

Household Stories of the Brothers Grimm by Jacob Grimm

My Name Is J J and others in the series by Brookie B. Dickerson

Landing of the Pilgrims by James Daugherty

Little House in the Big Wood and others in the series by Laura
 Ingalls Wilder

Little Women or Little Men by Louisa Alcott

Nancy Drew series by Carolyn Keene

Mary Poppins or others in the series by P. L. Travers

Ramona the Pest and other Ramona titles by Beverly Cleary

Robinson Crusoe by Daniel Defoe

Some Merry Adventures of Robin Hood by Howard Pyle

The Boy's King Arthur by Sir Thomas Malory

The Fables of Aesop by Aesop

The Hardy Boys series by Franklin W. Dixon

The Hobbit by J. R. R. Tolkien

The Indian in the Cupboard series by Lynne Reid Banks

Treasure Island by Robert L. Stevenson

The author of the following short story is unknown, but his message to parents is worth reading again and again:

One morning my small son said to me at breakfast, "Daddy, may I read to you? I got nine out of ten for reading at school yesterday."

"Very good," said I, hardly glancing from my morning paper.

"May I?"

"Eh? May you what?" I demanded, being in haste and wishful to glance over the news and finish breakfast in next to no time.

"May I read to you?"

"Well, not now son! There's no time."

So off I went to catch a bus.

Home that evening, I told my little son that I would listen to his reading as soon as I had my supper. But somebody called, and I had to see him. And finally I went into my son's bedroom, and found him fast asleep, his cheeks wet with tears, a school reader open on his bed. Thus through this experience, I learned my lesson: to show my love for him a little more and for myself a little less."

Writing

It is important for kids to learn to express themselves through writing. Writing in a journal or diary allows them to practice their penmanship, their grammar and their ability to express themselves. It also provides great satisfaction when they later re-read their life stories. A pattern of journal writing leads adults to record important events, lessons and feelings for later generations.

Letters to grandparents, cousins and friends are also excellent opportunities to develop writing skills. A quick email message cannot replace a more personal handwritten letter, thank you note or sympathy note. Such habits should start early.

Consider having the kids interview Grandma or Grandpa. The kids can make a list of questions beforehand, then record the answers on a camcorder, computer or cassette recorder to preserve Grandma and Grandpa's voices. Later they can write a short report in their journal or diary. They could also interview Mom or Dad about their work or about an important event in their life.

You could teach your kids basic poetry concepts, have them read poetry or have them write a poem about themselves, about their pet or about an aspect of Nature.

Memorizing

Memorization is an extremely helpful skill and is worth practicing. Possible activities in this area include reciting poetry, learning a song, rehearsing the multiplication tables, learning the names of the states and memorizing quotations from great people. Younger children can recite the alphabet and older ones can be challenged to recite the alphabet backwards.

Music

Music has great power to stir emotions. It can soothe or excite, inspire or depress. In the words of William Congreve, "Music hath charms to soothe a savage breast, to soften rocks, or bend a knotted oak." Not everyone is born with an ear for pitch, but everyone can learn to appreciate music and to distinguish between different types. With experimentation, you can determine how your kids relate to music and can provide opportunities for them to develop their talents. I suggest that every family buy an instrument of some sort, at least a recorder (a type of flute), a harmonica, a guitar, or a basic electronic keyboard and encourage their kids to learn to play a tune. It would have been sad indeed if the great composers' parents had not discovered and developed their children's musical talent.

Summer goals can include practicing an instrument, composing a tune, memorizing a song or just learning to identify a certain type of music. Use this opportunity for you and your child to understand the child's music preferences and capabilities. You might set a goal one summer to explore five types of music such as jazz, rap, Latin American, rock, marches, ballads, or classical music. Then ask for an analysis and preferences from the child. If they show an interest in performing music, practice and/or performing goals can be set.

Most of our kids were blessed with musical talent and one of our priorities was to provide them all with piano lessons. This was a sacrifice because of the cost, but it added to the good spirit in our home, allowed each of the kids to learn their capabilities and permitted them to develop a skill that will bless their own families for a lifetime. Their skills vary, but all of our kids can at least play church hymns and some are quite proficient. The girls also extended their music interest to stringed instruments (violin, viola or cello) and we provided an inexpensive instrument to each of them so they could continue to develop and enjoy their talents after high school.

We were fortunate to have a good orchestra and band program and did not initially have to buy instruments nor pay for lessons. If your school does not have a music program, you may be able to get lessons from a local music store or private teacher. Your community may even have a youth band or orchestra. If your budget will not permit you to buy an instrument, you might consider renting one.

Performing can be a frightening experience and the safest place to practice performing should be in the home. Whatever your kids accomplish with music, have them perform for you or for the entire family. A talent night where everyone in the family performs can reduce the 'opening night jitters' for shy ones. With a little praise, even shy kids can become excellent performers because they often prepare better than those who are overly confident.

A jar of M&Ms can be a helpful tool for rewarding young children for music practice time. For example, if they are learning a song, give an M&M or two each time they practice through the song. Remember "... a spoonful of sugar helps the medicine go down . . ." In teaching a group song, have each one perfect the song on his own, rewarding them individually before putting the group together.

Sewing

When I was growing up, sewing was required in junior high and high school. I had excellent teachers who taught me well. It is a skill I have appreciated throughout my life and have enjoyed immensely. Sewing clothes for my kids helped a great deal with our budget. Today many schools no longer provide classes in cooking and sewing and fewer children learn these skills at home. Even learning to sew a straight seam will allow your kids to make fundamental curtains or pillowcases, to sew quilt squares together, or to repair torn clothes. You can often find inexpensive used sewing machines for beginners. I recommend a used name brand machine over a new machine of lesser quality. Beginning sewing classes are often offered at fabric stores during the summer.

If you start your kids with easier projects, such as pillowcases or beanbags, they can develop the confidence to tackle something more challenging. Shorts, aprons, pajamas and basic purses are easy second stage ideas. Remember that each skill learned provides the basis for the next. It is tempting to choose a darling pattern that is too difficult. If it is too challenging, discouragement comes quickly, especially if it is not turning out like the picture on the pattern, and sewing will no longer be fun or rewarding.

You can find elementary patterns at a nearby fabric store. Do not expect perfection at first, but patiently resolve each challenge. Start with inexpensive fabrics so the cost of errors will not add frustration. As your kids progress, they can have the satisfaction of making excellent clothing for themselves and as gifts.

We established very early the expectation that our girls' high school graduation gift would be a sewing machine (and that our boys would receive a set of handyman tools). We knew that if they did not have a sewing machine, they would not continue to sew. Our girls have rich childhood memories of shopping for patterns and fabric with their mother. Since then they have sewn play clothes and Halloween costumes for their children, curtains, and some of their own clothes, saving money and giving them access to unique styles and pleasant memories. A few have even made evening gowns, lined jackets and dress shirts.

Quilting

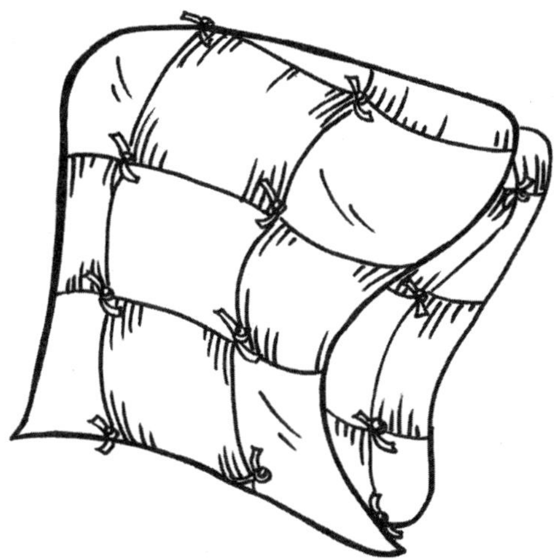

Through the years all of our family members have enjoyed making quilts, talking and laughing as we worked. I refer here to full-sized quilts sewn by hand with quilting frames, not the kind sewn by machine or by one person alone. There are many books and magazines on the subject of quilting, some available online. With a little

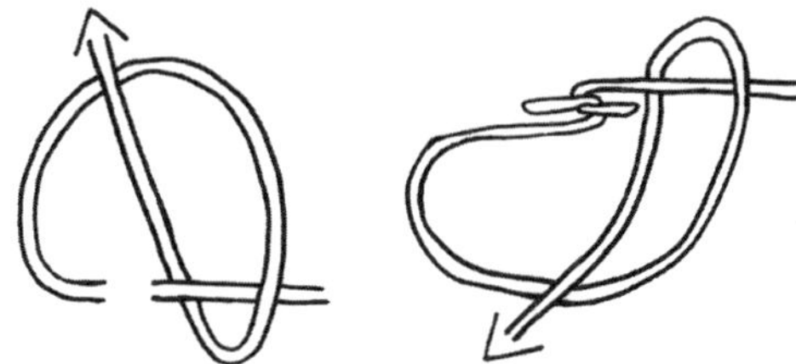

scouting around, you may find a friend willing to loan their quilting frames to you for a couple of weeks. Frames can also be purchased from the Grace Company at www.sewvacdirect.com or from Vonda's Quilt Frames at www.quiltframes.com. The simplest quilts are made from two bed sheets and a roll of batting, which is the insulating material. Batting may be purchased from a fabric store.

Stitching can be rather complex or quite basic. We generally used a long running stitch (over and under at about half inch intervals) with a double strand of crochet thread on a large needle. Occasionally we 'tied' a quilt, working from right to left, making a short stitch about every six inches and tying a square knot in the thread before making the next stitch. The thread was then cut halfway between stitches (see illustration). Tied quilts have fluffy tufts of yarn at every knot. As the outer parts of the project are stitched, the frames are rolled and re-clamped so the inner parts can be reached. The edges of the quilt may be 'bound' by rolling one side over the other and sewing by hand or by machine.

I suggest that you start by making a small tied quilt for a baby or young child and then try a more challenging project. The most important elements are to have fun and to make the quilt together.

Chapter 6
Other Fun Ideas For Summer

If a child is to keep alive his inborn sense of wonder,
he needs the companionship of at least one adult who can share it,
rediscovering with him the joy, excitement and mystery
of the world we live in.
—Rachel Carson, The Sense of Wonder

There is so much you can do in the summer! Here are some ideas that will enrich family relationships while providing pleasant times together and an opportunity to learn.

A Simple Play

Set a date when Grandpa and Grandma, aunts and uncles, or friends and neighbors can join you for an evening. You can write your own dialogue for a well-known story and include each member of the family in the cast. If you need more participants, invite friends or neighbors to join in. We enjoyed presenting classic stories such as:

The Three Little Pigs
The Little Red Hen
Goldilocks and the Three Bears
The Three Billy Goats Gruff

Refer to Appendix B for complete scripts for these four stories. These scripts are basic and are meant to prompt your own creativity, adapting them to suit your family. You may want to make participation in a play a summer goal as part of a talent night performed for family and friends. The talent night may also include music that family members have learned as summer goals, whether sung, played on the piano, or played on other instruments. It is always more motivational to be working for a special night, so set the date far enough ahead to give plenty of time to prepare and to anticipate. None of this should overwhelm you if you keep it simple. Let all the family participate and take it one step at a time. You and your kids will have a great time together.

Scenery can be made from cardboard refrigerator boxes or poster board. For example, if you are going to perform *The Three Little Pigs*, get a refrigerator box from an appliance store. Cut down each edge of the box leaving four large, rectangular cardboard pieces. Draw a straw house, a stick house, and a brick house on three pieces of the cardboard. From the fourth piece of cardboard, make a large black pot for the wolf to fall into. The first little pig holds the straw house, the second little pig holds the stick house, and the third little pig holds the brick house.

The person performing the part of the wolf comes to the first house and says his part: "Little pig, little pig let me come in!" The pig says, "Not by the hair of my chinny chin chin!" The big bad wolf then says, "Then I'll huff and I'll puff and I'll blow your house in!" So he huffs and he puffs and blows the house in. As the wolf does that, the first little pig lets his straw house fall down and runs to join the pig in the stick house. The wolf then goes through the same dialogue with the second little pig after which the two little pigs join the third little pig in the brick house.

See Appendix B for more detailed suggestions and full scripts for all four mini-dramas.

Costumes are easily made from construction paper for ears, noses, and tails. Bow ties around the neck add a great touch. Use your imagination. Your production can be as big or as small as you choose and there is no right or wrong. The kids love the creativity and it brings confidence in memorizing, performing, and working together. It takes a bit of effort, but you will be glad that you did it. Remember to have the video camera handy because you will definitely want to save this for future viewing.

Crafts

Children love modeling clay. The recipe below is for a good, non-toxic play dough that is easy to clean up and can be kept for weeks in the refrigerator.

Recipe for "Play Dough"

This play dough keeps children busy for long periods of time!

    1½ level Tablespoons powdered alum or cream of tartar

    ½ cup salt

    2½ cups flour

    3 Tablespoons oil

    2 cups water

    Food coloring

Bring the oil, water and food coloring just to a boil and remove from heat. Sift in the dry ingredients. Mix thoroughly and let cool. Between uses, if stored in refrigerator in an airtight container, play dough will keep for several weeks.

An old broom handle cut into eight inch lengths makes several excellent rolling pins. A set of small cookie cutters is a fun addition.

Here are some other crafts for younger children.

- Make anything from construction paper, glue and tape.
- Glue paper rings into a chain.
- Draw stick figures, add clothing and color.
- Glue colored macaroni on paper to make pictures or designs.
- Make figures, people and animals from pipe cleaners.
- Make paper airplanes.
- Make fruit loop necklaces (see the Chapter 7 on traveling).
- Let a child pound nails into a board.
- Glue craft sticks together to create gifts, home decorations or holiday items.

Kids over ten years of age often enjoy crafts that require tools. Safety dictates that a parent supervise many of these activities. See the Cub Scout materials provided by the Boy Scouts of America or comparable materials by the Girl Scouts of America. Most cities have a local store that carries scout materials. Scout supplies may also be ordered online at www.scouting.org or www.girlscouts.org. Many Web sites offer additional ideas and some give detailed instructions. More ideas follow:

- Bird house
- Soapbox racer or cub mobile
- Sun dial
- Origami paper figures
- Kite
- Model airplane
- Pinewood Derby car (ask permission to race with a local Cub Scout pack)
- Three-piece paddle boat with elastic wind-up paddle
- Paper airplanes
- Wind chimes

More crafts for kids of all ages.

- Decorate a small box, bottle or plastic container by gluing to the sides pictures cut from magazines. Use the resulting containers for pencils, toys or wastebaskets.

- Make a scrapbook from a three-ring binder and heavy bond paper or construction paper. Glue in pictures of yourself, friends and relatives, places you have visited, programs from important events and even advertisements for things you own or would like to have. Label the pictures and write a bit about them.

- Draw a picture, color it, and then cut it into pieces to make a puzzle. Have another family member do the same and then trade puzzles. Challenge Grandma or Grandpa to put the puzzle together. When you are finished with the puzzle, glue the pieces on stiff construction paper or poster board and hang the resulting picture on the bedroom door.

- Make a collage with a theme such as cartoons, people, animals, etc. Cut examples from newspapers or old magazines and glue them onto construction paper or poster board.

- Make caterpillar creatures. Cut an egg carton lengthwise and decorate with pipe cleaner antennas, glitter, paint, cotton balls, or whatever.

- Create a piñata or face mask from paper mache'. Mix a paste from flour and water, about the consistency of applesauce. Then tear strips of newspaper, dip them in the paste, and place them over an inflated balloon. Add strips to make the desired form and allow to dry overnight. Then paint the form as desired. The paste can be messy, so apply it over spread-out newspaper on the garage floor, lawn, or porch.

- Document the family's hand sizes. Mix Plaster of Paris with water to the consistency of peanut butter. Make one inch deep forms by cutting out the bottom of used plastic bottles such as milk bottles. Pour one half inch of the mix into each form and press each person's hand into the mix. Using a nail or sharp stick, letter the owner's name and the year next to each handprint. Let dry overnight. Paint if desired.

- Make pasta jewelry. Start with dry macaroni or other pasta and string it on yarn. Then paint the pasta with tempera paint or dip in food coloring. Food coloring stains badly, so hang it over a spread-out newspaper on the porch, garage floor or lawn until the pasta dries. This appeals more to younger children.

- Make jewelry with materials from a craft store. You can purchase a wide variety of beads, shapes, letters, charms and other materials for bracelets, necklaces and other jewelry.

- Make puppets from paper sacks or from old socks.

- Make a nature plaque. Stain a block of wood with furniture stain or shoe polish and let it dry. Then glue on a design of seeds, sticks, small rocks, nuts, leaves or any natural thing.

- Make vegetable prints. Cut designs into a piece of potato or carrot and use a ink stamp pad or dish of tempera paint to make a pattern of prints on paper. This makes a personalized paper for wrapping gifts or even a nice wall hanging.

- Make a special card for a friend or relative. It might say "Thank you," or "I'm glad you're my friend," or "Sorry to hear you are sick—get well soon," or another appropriate comment. Make more than one card. This activity only requires construction paper, glue, crayons and scissors.

- Make Christmas gifts, decorations or ornaments in July. Ideas are readily available at crafts shops, from books at the library, and from friends. A few examples: clothes pin reindeer or soldiers, felt figures, wreaths, pom-pom animals, candy canes made with pipe cleaners, and personalized pillowcases using fabric markers or puff paints.

Music

A key element of music is rhythm or the 'beat.' You might make instruments for a rhythm band and march through the house beating a rhythm (one, two, three, four . . . one, two, three, four . . . etc.) in time with your feet.

For this two blocks can be hit together, a spoon can be banged on a metal pot lid, or you may blow over the mouth of a bottle partially filled with water. Feel free to use your imagination.

Another alternative is to make your own set of hand-held pipe chimes. With a set of pipe chimes, kids can experience differences in pitch, volume, and timing. As the family plays together, kids also learn teamwork. Chimes can be used to make basic chord accompaniments for popular tunes, hymns and kids' songs. Singing groups will enjoy accompanying themselves. We gave a set of chimes to each of our kids and they report that they have used and enjoyed them often, especially at Christmas.

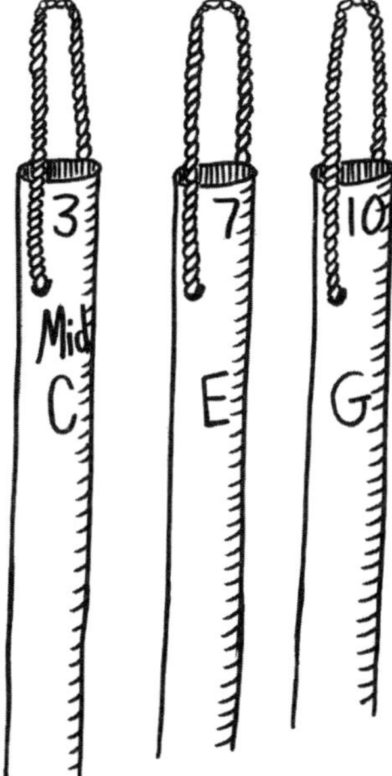

Playing all the chimes usually requires eleven people, each holding one chime, but smaller groups can also enjoy playing the seven basic chimes (those with colors) numbered two through twelve. As few as four people can play this reduced basic set by holding two chimes in one hand and shaking a mallet between them so that both chimes are being struck. Basic instructions for making pipe chimes follow and additional information and sample music is provided in Appendix C.

Chime #	Note	Length (Inches)	Color Marks	Chord #
1	B flat	13-3/8		
2	B	13	red, purple	V7, II
3	C (mid)	12-5/8	blue, yellow	IV, I
4	C sharp	12-1/4		
5	D	11-7/8	red, purple	V7, II
6	E flat	11-1/2		
7	E	11-1/4	yellow	I
8	F	10-7/8	blue, red	IV, V7
9	F sharp	10-11/16		
10	G	10-3/8	yellow, red, purple	I, V7, II
11	A flat	9-7/8		
12	A	9-9/16	blue	IV
13	B flat	9-3/8		
14	B	9-3/16	red, purple	V7, II
15	C (high)	8-7/8	blue, yellow	IV, I
16	C sharp	8-5/8		
17	D	8-5/16	red, purple	V7, II
18	E flat	8-1/8		
19	E	7-7/8	yellow	I

Other fun activities with music:

- Attend a musical event regularly. For example, you might attend all or most of the city's band or orchestra concerts during a season. Many communities have free concerts in the park during the summer and high school bands and orchestras have several concerts during the school year. Regional jazz or folk music festivals often last for several days and feature many types of music. Look online or call a local radio station or newspaper.

- Learn to sing rounds. *Row, Row, Row Your Boat, Three Blind Mice,* and *Little Tom Tucker* are popular songs that can be sung as a round. Others may be found online. Rounds are difficult but not impossible for little ones and are greatly rewarding, especially when there are only one or two people in each group. Be sure to perform for family or friends.

Games and Other Activities

There are many excellent games that families may enjoy together. Keep in mind that members of the family have different interests and time availability. Mom and Dad are often tired at the end of the day and weekends can be full also, so some families will be less inclined to buy a game that normally takes several hours. For others, a long game allows more strategy and relaxation. Youth enjoy active games but can get silly after a bit, so a second or third game may get out of hand. It is often best to let participants know how much time you have available before you start the activity. Taking turns choosing the game or movie will reduce conflicts and teach cooperation.

Here are some good ideas for summer activities:

- Assemble a puzzle. Puzzles are entertaining and educational for the whole family. Even young children are able to assemble a twenty-five or sixty piece puzzle once they understand what is expected. Sorting and assembling puzzles helps develop reasoning and analytical thinking.

- Have a Movie Marathon as a reward or for a special rest time. On a given day, let each of the kids rent a movie of their choice and then bring out pillows and blankets. Pop popcorn to eat on the blankets (for easy cleanup) and cut up apples to go along with it.

- Let the kids plan a treasure hunt, either for indoors or outdoors. Notes can lead from one location to another until the hunter finds the treasure.

- Build a fort in the family room by hanging sheets or blankets over card tables, chairs, or couches. Ignore the mess and leave the fort up for two or three days. Join the kids for a card game or story in the fort.

- Play ball. Besides baseball, try ping pong, foam ball badminton, regular "catch" or "keep away," basketball, or dodge ball.

- Have a running competition. Mom or Dad joining in makes this fun for the kids. Tie legs together for a three-legged race. Sack races and wheelbarrow races are great, too.

- Try horseshoes, darts (wall or Velcro type), basketball throw, beanbag toss, Frisbee football (requires at least four people), archery, marbles, etc. To make it fair, handicap the older and more capable family members by requiring them to use left hands, close one eye, etc.

- Play "Steal The Bacon." Make two lines by placing ropes or strings on the ground about twenty to thirty feet apart. Tie a rag or small towel into a knot and place it halfway between the lines. Divide into even teams and designate a referee. The referee calls a member of each team to stand behind their line. When the referee says "go," the two run to the middle and with fakes and strategy try to grab the "bacon" and return behind their line without being touched by the other player. If a player gets home with the bacon without being touched, they call for a member of the other team to join their team. Likewise, if a player tags his opponent while they are stealing the bacon, the unsuccessful thief joins the opposing team. If a player touches either the bacon or the opponent when the opponent does not have the bacon, the "toucher" is "it" and can be tagged out unless they grab the bacon and return to their line without being touched. The game ends when all players are on one team.

- Have a home dancing class. A parent can teach their favorite style of dancing, the older kids can teach their style, or simply dance as desired to the music.

- Have a lazy day at the end of summer. After a productive summer and when chores are completed, one of our daughters sets aside a day before school begins, separate from summer goals rewards, in which no jobs are required.

- Play Jacks, Marbles, Four Square, Hopscotch, or Jump Rope. I enjoyed these games as a child and they are now staging a come-back. See Appendix D for the history and instructions for each.

Outside the Home

Summertime is a great time to keep kids active and fit. While I recommend that sports be balanced with other important activities, sports also provide physical and social development and teach teamwork and self-discipline. Physical activity is also a good alternative to TV and video game time. Check your city and YMCA for available programs. You may find it helpful to arrange carpooling with friends or neighbors to help with transportation.

While I was raising my kids our city had a great program of water sports which was available for all ages at a reasonable cost. We started with "Mom and Tot" classes and the children progressed to two-week-long swim classes in the mornings. Our next step was team competitions in swimming, diving and synchronized swimming, depending on the individual's interest.

Afternoon or evening swimming at the community pool became a reward for completing family chores. I enjoyed going with the kids because it also helped me stay fit. Kids love to have someone there to appreciate all their new tricks.

More ideas for summer fun outside the home:

- Grow a garden. Have the kids plant a corner of your yard or just a few pots on your porch. Flowers or vegetables will show the kids the miracle of plant growth and give them an opportunity to be responsible for watering and weeding.

- Go to a park and play ball or just enjoy the swings.

- Have a dollar store mini-spree. Give each of the kids a few dollars to spend any way they like. Do not rush them but have a time limit. Let them really explore and search for what they want. Have each one explain their choice, including at least one item they decided against. This allows them to explore their own preferences, helps develop decision-making skills and teaches them about consequences.

- Go to a dairy and watch the milking process. Call ahead for permission to see the cows being milked.

- Visit a farm. If you show interest, many farmers will tell you about their farm.

- Visit an airport. Park where you can see the runway and watch landings and takeoffs or go inside the terminal and explore. On several occasions, I spread a blanket on a grassy spot at the end of the runway for our small, local airport. The small kids and I spent a pleasant hour or so enjoying a special snack and watching the small planes take off and land. Since 9-11 security restrictions prohibit parking at the very end of the runway, but we have observed airport operations from nearby hills and from parking garages. Check with the Transportation Safety Authority if you have further questions.

- Visit an elderly person in your neighborhood. Take an item that you or the kids have made such as cookies, a fruit salad, a paper flower bouquet or a bouquet of fresh flowers. Have the kids sing a few songs that they have learned. Elderly people especially like the company. Consider visiting a nursing home or hospital.

- Visit relatives or friends whom you have not seen for a while.

- Visit a roadside fruit stand and let the kids choose a fresh yummy item. If the fruit stand is near its parent farm, show the kids where the fruit comes from and perhaps some of the farm equipment. If you live near an operating fruit or nut orchard, ask if you can pick your own. Picking grapes, peaches, cherries and apples has been a frequent memory-maker for our family.

- Ride somewhere on the city bus. Explore a new part of town to see a movie, concert or museum.

- If your city has a zoo, visit often and "adopt" one of the animals. Note changes in your chosen subject and, back at home, learn about their native habitat and favorite food.

School Kids' Surprise Adventure

Have a School Kids Surprise Adventure. My husband and I always praised the kids for their school performance. Many parents reward good grades with money, but because we had a large family and since the kids did well in school, it would have cost us a fortune. Also we did not feel good placing an emphasis on money as the reward for doing well. So when our oldest was still young, we began the tradition of having a very nice surprise activity at the end of the school year in recognition of their academic efforts.

Despite considerable planning on our part, we kept the destination of the activity a secret until the night before, but carefully briefed everyone on the time to be reserved and the appropriate attire. We hired a baby sitter for the younger children so my husband and I could both attend. The special nature of the event was highlighted by the mystery, by Mom and Dad's careful planning, by our setting aside the time to do it together, and by the special appreciation for school performance that we expressed at the end.

One year we spent an entire day at a water park, had a delicious picnic there, and finished with a movie at a theatre. Another year we had a wonderful day floating down the river on inner tubes, eating our lunch along the way. Another time we bicycled several miles along a canal bank to the river where it began, had a picnic under a large tree and returned with a downhill ride through a beautiful part of town. Once, when the kids were older, we drove a couple of hours to another city, stayed in a hotel, enjoyed the hotel pool, visited an airplane museum, and watched pay-per-view movies in our hotel room.

One of our daughters said recently that the School Kids Surprise Adventure was one of the absolute highlights of the summer. Choose whatever works for your family and your budget.

Family Night

Perhaps the most powerful concept we can recommend for strengthening the family is to set aside one night a week as a Family Night. This applies throughout the year, not only during the summer. A regular family night requires particular devotion by parents because of the constant pressures from outside the home, but the rewards can be tremendous. Set aside a day and time and use that time faithfully for a family council on issues of interest to all. Family Night provides a reserved time for such things as the weekly calendar, family mini-classes, a talent night, a special report, a family activity, or an inspirational thought. Family members take turns preparing the special thought or activity.

We allowed the kids to take turns choosing the refreshments within a budget, either a homemade treat or one from the store. Part of the fun was one-on-one time with Dad on the way to buy the ingredients for the refreshments. The great memories associated with our Family Nights are never-ending and we are pleased to see our kids doing the same with their families.

Chapter 7
Making Road Trips Fun For Everyone

*"How you spend your time is more important
than how you spend your money.
Money mistakes can be corrected, but time is gone forever."*
—Author Unknown

Challenges

Since we have always lived quite a distance from my family, each summer we would find ourselves packing up the car or van and heading back to the farm. It generally took about twelve hours on the road each way. These trips were made long before there were DVD players in vans or portable video games. In spite of these inventions, I find myself looking back and being grateful that these newfangled toys were not an option. Time in the car is invaluable time spent together. You can have the undivided attention of your kids since no one can get away! You may want an occasional movie on a long trip if you have such equipment, but there are many things to learn and to do in the car that can provide great memories and draw families closer together.

Activities

Alphabet Sign Game

Find letters of the alphabet on signs outside the car. If the kids are old enough, this can be done silently. We generally excluded license plates and signs on vehicles except where there were few signs. Each person is on their honor to see the letters clearly and to take credit for them only while looking at the sign and in proper order. Younger children can play the game aloud with a parent helping them identify letters.

Fruit Loop Necklaces

One of our favorite traveling activities for young children was to string Fruit Loops. Many otherwise boring hours have been made pleasant this way. We found that children as young as three years, confined in a moving vehicle, can often be entertained for an hour or more making Fruit Loop necklaces and bracelets. For many, eating the Fruit Loop jewelry occupies another hour. Even teens enjoy this activity.

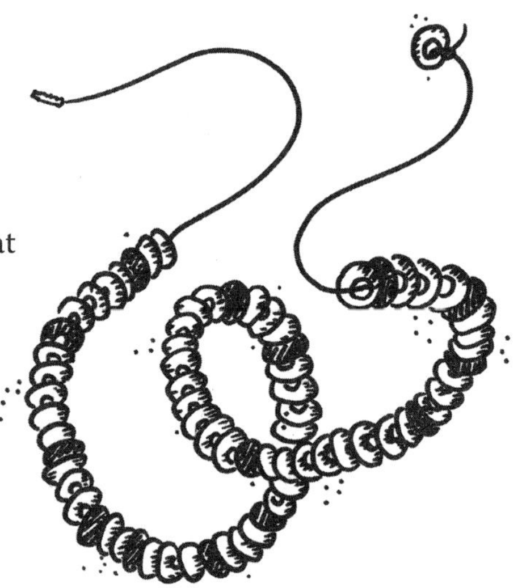

Fruit Loop Necklaces

Cut a piece of yarn to an appropriate length and put a piece of scotch tape around the end to reinforce the yarn so it will go through the fruit loop holes. As an alternative, tie a piece of waxed dental floss to the end of the yarn as a makeshift needle. Fill a paper cup with Fruit Loops and simply feed them one at a time onto the string. Cheerios have less sugar but the holes are not as large and, in our experience, children prefer the colorful, tasty Fruit Loops.

Math Game

Start by stating a math question such as, "add two and seven." Then continue with other math steps geared to the ability of the kids involved, giving adequate time to make the calculations. After five or six steps, ask for the answer. This can be done with or without paper and pencil.

Alphabet Trip Game

Play the Alphabet Trip game. Say, "I am going on a trip and I am going to take an item beginning with the letter "a" (such as "apple."). The next person says, "I am going on a trip and I am going to take an apple and something beginning with the letter "b" (such as "boot"). The next person says, "I am going on a trip and I am going to take an apple, a boot (repeat all previous items) and something beginning with the letter "c". You continue on with each person in the car until you have completed the entire alphabet. This tests your memory and is fun, especially if you take outlandish items such as a spaceship or a moonbeam. A variation of this game is to add any item in no particular order (not alphabetical).

Finger Weaving

With a skein of yarn, finger weaving can keep a child busy for hours. You can use the woven yarn for girls' hair ribbons, for decorations, for play ropes or just for the satisfaction of weaving something. Baby yarn makes a more delicate hair ribbon, white glittery yarn makes a beautiful Christmas garland, and butcher string makes a rather strong rope. This activity is best for ages five or older, depending on the child's attention span, and is well worth the minor expense for materials.

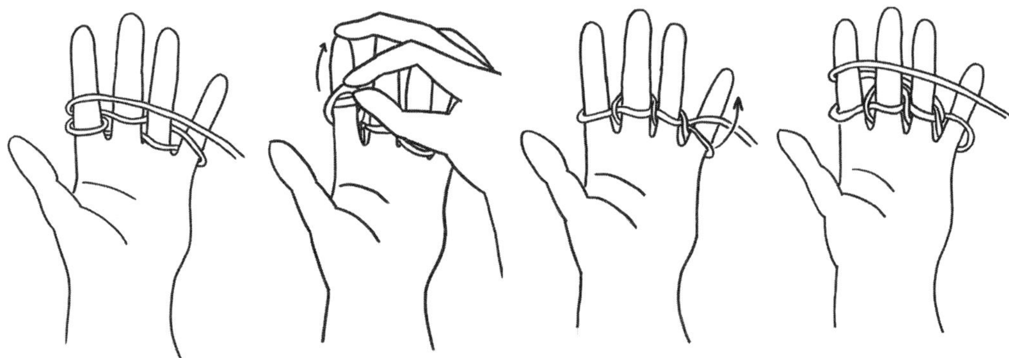

Instructions for Finger Weaving

Upturn your left palm and, with your right hand loop the end of the yarn (the "tail") once around your forefinger (nearest the thumb) in a clockwise direction (so the long end of the yarn goes behind the second finger – see the illustration on page 57). With your right hand, weave the yarn between your fingers, alternating front and back. After passing your smallest finger, loop around that finger and continue alternating around your fingers to the left, finally laying the yarn across all of the fingers as shown in the illustration. With your right hand and starting with the forefinger, pull the lower loop (in front of each finger, nearest the palm) over the tip of each finger, crossing the straight yarn. Then, with your right hand, pull the loose yarn behind your fingers and across the front of your fingers as before. With your right hand, again pull the lower loop over each finger, crossing the straight yarn. Then again pull the loose yarn behind your fingers and across the front of your fingers as before. Continue pulling the loose yarn around your hand and extending the lower loops over each finger, making the woven ribbon as long as desired. Periodically, pull on the tail end of the yarn to tighten the ribbon. The tail end of the ribbon will look better if it is tied with an overhand knot and the loose end trimmed off. A long ribbon can be cut to any length after tying a knot to prevent unraveling.

Singing Time

Adopt a favorite song and sing it often and with gusto. We would sing *I've Been Working on the Railroad* whenever we were tired or cranky or just bored. Everyone knew the song and joined in, perhaps with a little harmony or just with a variation. Traveling is also an excellent time to learn a new song, to practice singing rounds, or to memorize a part for an upcoming church or school program. You may be able to find good sing along tapes or CDs for kids at the local library. "Veggie Tales" is a good example or you may choose to buy some at a bookstore and develop your own music library.

A Crocheted Dishcloth

If I were making a long car trip today, I might have the kids crochet a pot holder or dishcloth instead of a slipper. Slippers are not as popular now and everyone needs a good dishcloth. Also, crocheting is easier to teach and projects move more quickly.

Basic Double Crocheted Dishcloth

For basic instructions on how to crochet and other easy patterns, see http://www.crochet.about.com.

Materials:

Worsted weight cotton yarn, any color (a small skein makes one, a large spool makes several)

Size G or H crochet hook

Finished size: 10 inch square. If yours ends up smaller or larger, it's okay since a dishcloth can be any size.

Start by leaving a six inch length of yarn hanging while making the dishcloth. Weave this length in when the dishcloth is finished to secure the end so it won't unravel.

Chain 30.

Row 1: Double crochet (d.c.) in the third chain from the hook and d.c. in each chain across. Turn and chain two. (29 d.c.)

Row 2: D.c.in first loop and continue across. Turn and chain two.

Repeat row 2. Continue to d.c. until you reach the length that you want the dishcloth to be. I like it to be square.

Finish off and weave in the ends.

If you want a smaller dishcloth, chain less at the beginning. If every row grows narrower, you may be missing the first stitch or the last, so count stitches often to assure the same number in each row. When double crocheting the two chains at the beginning of each row, count as a double crochet. This pattern can be made with single crochet if you find it easier, but I prefer double crocheting because it works up faster.

Row, Row, Row Your Boat

Sing *Row, Row, Row Your Boat* several times, leaving off the last word each time until there are no more words. For example:

Round One

Row, row, row your boat, gently down the stream.

Merrily, merrily, merrily, merrily, life is but a dream.

Round Two

Row, row, row your boat, gently down the stream.

Merrily, merrily, merrily, merrily, life is but a. . .

Round Three

Row, row, row your boat, gently down the stream.

Merrily, merrily, merrily, merrily, life is but . . .

You Name It

To play You Name It, Dad or Mom says something like this: "Name three states that begin with the letter N," such as New York, New Jersey, North Carolina, etc. Each child in the car tries to be the first to fulfill the request. The parent may then say, "Name two cities that start with the letter M," such as Minneapolis, Memphis, Milwaukee, etc. and the kids compete to fulfill the request. Dad or Mom may then say, "Name two countries beginning with the letter C," such as Columbia, Canada, Chile, etc. Geography is a good category for one age group, while fruits and vegetables, plants, animals, or insects may be best for another. If chosen to be challenging but not too hard, this game can entertain the entire family for many miles.

Guess the Time or Guess the Mileage Contest

This is great fun. Choose a destination, perhaps the next major city, which will be reached in less than an hour. Have a contest to guess your exact arrival time. One of the kids can be the official timer, recording the destination and the guessed times for everyone in the car, and announcing the winner when you arrive. A variation of this game is to guess the odometer reading.

Dollar Store Pit Stop

While on your trip and passing by one of the many Dollar Stores, stop for a few minutes. Give each of the kids a dollar and a time limit and let them choose whatever they want. Anticipating the stop and later exploring their purchase in the car can brighten a tiring trip.

Scavenger Hunt for the Car

This activity requires a little advance preparation. Think of your travel route and make a list of items the children might see along the way. Make drawings if the children cannot yet read. Examples might include:

- Windmill
- Cactus
- Pine tree
- Pickup truck
- Cow
- Wildflowers
- Bird
- Bridge
- ATV
- Semi-truck
- Sheep
- Volkswagen Beetle

The goal is to check off each item or picture on the list as many times as they are seen. Mom can even hand out stickers, which young children love, to mark the items found. Children can look for items on the list during the entire trip.

Seat Belt Surprise

We live in a day and age in which seat belts are a must. An incentive for kids to wear their seat belts is the Seat Belt Surprise. Occasionally, not often, call out, "Seat Belt Surprise." Whoever is wearing their seat belt gets a piece of candy or a quarter. You might explain in the beginning that wearing a seat belt is being responsible and an occasional reward is great, but that we should always be responsible. Being responsible is its own reward. This positive approach usually brings better results than a scolding for not wearing a seat belt.

Read a Story or Listen to an Audio Book

Take along a supply of books such as those recommended for bedtime. Kids respond well to a longer story that can be read in installments, especially an adventure story that will hold their attention. This can also be a great time for the kids to read to each other. Elementary school kids love to read out loud to an audience. Older kids will enjoy a mystery story or an audio book, but younger children often lose interest. Resist the temptation to listen to an audio book that only the adults will enjoy.

Make Up a Story

A good creative activity is to make up your own story. The first person could start with something like this: "One warm summer evening just as the sun was going down . . ." Then the next person adds a sentence or two. Everyone takes turns until you reach a reasonable finish to the story. Accept everyone's imaginative input and let the story develop. You may be surprised at the creativity of your kids as the story takes its comical and interesting turns.

Keep a Travel Log or Write Postcards

If kids can write, they often enjoy keeping a travel log during the trip, either in a diary or on separate pages. They can record what they saw, what they liked most, or what they will do when they arrive home. This can also be a good time to write letters or postcards to friends back home.

Count Animals

While passing through an area with deer, rabbits, cows, horses, crows or other animals, count all the deer or rabbits or cows you can see. This works best where the animals are not too hard to see.

An Adventure Story

I relate the following experience to encourage families of all sizes to enjoy a travel adventure. Planning and preparation are certainly required, but the rewards are very much worth the time and effort.

Several years ago we made a goal to take our kids on a long road trip before our older kids started to leave home. We had learned that the best chance for success with a major activity or project was to plan well in advance, maintaining flexibility for changing circumstances. So five years before our oldest child graduated from high school, we began planning.

At that time we were living in the western part of the country. Because we had lived in the eastern states early in our marriage and because we wanted our kids to see as much of the country as possible, we decided to drive to the east coast and back, a four week long trip. Our goal was to travel across the south, spend time in Washington D.C., go up the eastern coast to New York and to East Hartford, Connecticut, where two of the children were born, and on to Boston before heading home. Of course, we needed to see Niagara Falls, drive for a short distance in Canada and visit relatives and friends along the way.

At that time we had ten kids, ranging in age from two to seventeen. We all enjoyed camping so we decided to camp along the way. We already had a large van and after careful shopping we added a modest travel trailer. By utilizing both the van and the trailer, we could bed everyone down. We bought portable radios so we could communicate between the two vehicles during the night.

We asked each of the school-age kids to choose a state through which we would be passing, send for information about that state and write a brief report about it, including places we might visit. To help the kids appreciate the trip more we had each one earn and contribute three times their age for gas money. They were gratified to know that their contributions paid for gas all the way to Tennessee. Involving the kids in the planning added more excitement for each of them and made them feel responsible.

My husband made reservations at several National Parks and other camping spots along the way and had a great itinerary planned. You can imagine that we needed many activities to keep the kids happy during the twelve days we spent actually driving in the van. To help occupy the time, I decided to teach the older kids how to knit, the goal being a pair of slippers. It kept them occupied for hours. By the time we got home, each of the kids, including our seven-year-old son, had knitted a pair of slippers.

Because we were self-contained, we were able to pull over for a quick potty stop in the trailer which had a bathroom. We were also able to fix lunch from our little stocked kitchen. We ate at fast food restaurants twice during the trip, but otherwise prepared all our own meals.

We visited historical sites and several great museums; picked strawberries; swam at beaches, lakes and pools; saw much of the beautiful USA; and stopped at the homes of friends and relatives, making a wonderfully successful trip. Our time together in the van was also rewarding, adding great memories of singing, knitting, and reading, playing games and enjoying activities together. Successful traveling can be achieved by creative thought and careful planning. You can do it!

Travel Ideas

Idea Box

Before a trip, put together an Idea Box—a box of items to have in the car for entertainment. Include a good supply of paper, tape, scissors, colored pencils or markers (be careful with crayons as they will melt in a hot car), workbooks, and coloring books. Make a list of oral games and paper and pencil games for later reference. With yarn, markers, stiff paper and a hole-punch, create "sewing cards" by drawing pictures and punching holes around the edges of the drawings through which the children can lace the yarn. You may want to include a few travel games, making a trip to a variety store for ideas. Travel versions of games such as Checkers, Connect Four, Battleship and miniature pinball machines are available for two to ten dollars. Long-lasting treats such as lollipops or Jolly Ranchers are also a good addition to your travel kit.

Child Activity Organizer

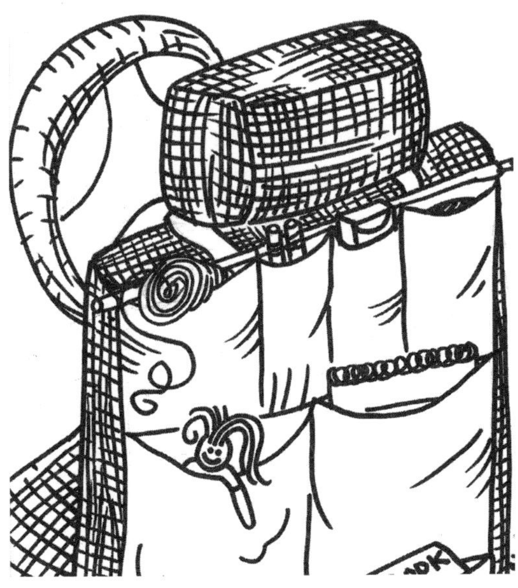

For long trips, buy or make a Child Activity Organizer. This set of cloth pouches hangs on the back of a car seat, providing a handy storage place for toys, books, paper, pencils, workbooks, and other things for the kids in the seat behind. Besides keeping things tidy and off the floor, kids learn to control their own environment. If you prefer not to make this item, a school day pack can be hung from the headrest of the seat in front, using string or ribbon to tie it there. (Instructions follow on page 66.)

Child Activity Organizer Directions

Purchase a ½" wooden dowel at least 42" long and two yards of light denim or medium weight fabric, 58-60" wide, enough for two car organizers. Cut the fabric according to the diagram on page 68, yielding:

(2) pieces 48" x 20" – backing
(6) pieces 12" x 20" – pockets
(4) pieces 3" x 60" – ties

The diagram is for 60" fabric. If 58" or 59" fabric is used, divide the width in thirds, making each organizer slightly less than 20" wide.

Step One

Fold over 2" and hem along the top 20" side of each of three 12" x 20" pocket pieces.

Step Two

Make the top pocket by placing a pocket piece, 2" hem at the top, along the 20" top of the backing, leaving 1-1/2" at the top of the backing for a ½" seam and a 1" wide casing for the wooden dowel. Fold under the bottom ½" of the pocket piece and sew to the backing. The bottom of the pocket should be 10-1/2" below the top of the backing. Then sew vertically down two places through the pocket and the backing to form three equally wide sections, each approximately 6-1/4" wide, with ¼" seams on the outside edges to secure the pocket to the backing.

Step Three

Make the middle pocket by placing a pocket piece (2" hem at the top) over the bottom of the top pocket. Fold under the bottom ½" of the pocket piece and sew to the backing (the bottom of the pocket should be 17" below the top of the backing).

Step Four

Make the bottom pocket by placing a pocket piece (2" hem at the top) over the bottom of the middle pocket. Fold under the bottom ½" of the pocket piece and sew to the backing (the bottom of the pocket should be 23-1/2" below the top of the backing). Now sew vertically down the middle of the middle and bottom pockets, attaching them to the backing and forming two equally wide sections. Finally, make ¼" seams on the outside edges to secure pockets to backing.

Step Five

Double each 3" x 60" strip to 1-1/2" wide, sew the long edge with a ¼" seam and turn inside out. Cut each tie in half. Finish the two ends by turning the ends in and sewing across. You will now have four ties.

Step Six

Align two ties vertically with their top ends even with the top of the front of the organizer, one tie 5" from the left outside edge of the organizer and the other tie 5" from the right outside edge, and pin the ties to the top of the organizer, folding the ties over the pockets. Align two other ties horizontally with their ends even with the side of the front of the organizer, one tie 3" above the bottom fold on the right side and one tie 3" above the bottom fold on the left side, and pin the ties to the edge of the organizer, folding the ties over the pockets. Fold the bottom 24" of the backing up over the pockets and ties, matching all edges, and sew a ½" seam along the sides of the organizer, leaving 1" open at the top of one side for the dowel casing and also leaving open the top edge between the ties. Turn the organizer inside out using the opening between the ties. Then stitch across the top to secure the opening in the top and sew just above the top pocket to form the dowel casing. Cut 21" from the wooden dowel and insert in the casing.

Step Seven

Attach to car seat with the ties, tying around the headrest and the bottom of the seat.

(Repeat for the second organizer.)

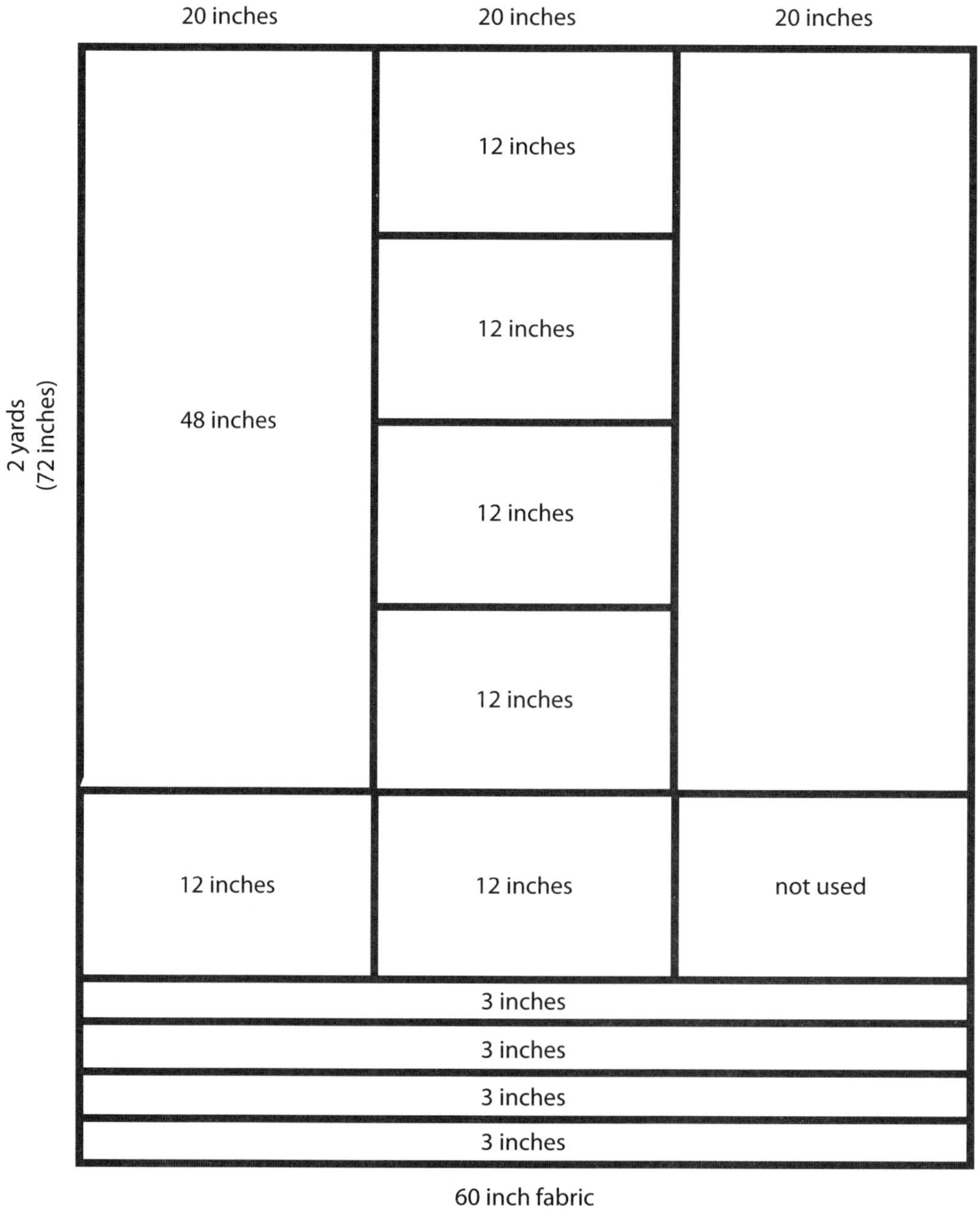

20 inches   20 inches   20 inches

2 yards
(72 inches)

48 inches

12 inches

12 inches

12 inches

12 inches

12 inches   12 inches   not used

3 inches

3 inches

3 inches

3 inches

60 inch fabric

Family Emergency 72-Hour Kit

One key to worry-free travel is to be prepared for challenges. If you have a few essentials you will be secure knowing that you can handle most emergencies. Always carry extra cash, drinking water, a blanket, a first aid kit and basic tools, including at least jumper cables, a pair of pliers, a small set of box-end wrenches and both Phillips and flat-head screwdrivers. Be sure your spare tire is in good condition and that you have a jack and tools to change a flat tire. Let family or neighbors know where you will be going and where you have reservations for the night. A pre-paid road service and a cell phone can be very helpful if the car breaks down. Carry road maps for the areas you will be visiting and know how to read them. You might consider always carrying a Family Emergency 72-hour Kit in the trunk of the car.

Family Emergency 72-Hour Kit Directions

- Phone numbers of key contacts (family, friends, Church leaders, community resources, work leaders)
- First aid kit, including anti-bacterial ointment, band-aids, gauze, tape, pain reliever, latex gloves, any medications needed regularly, Immodium (for diarrhea) and a laxative
- Foil blanket or sweater and a few diapers, if needed
- Food bars, hard candy, small can of meat (tuna, Spam, Vienna Sausages, dried meat, etc.), and infant formula, if needed
- Bottled water (at least two for each family member - refill when needed, reduces spread of disease to have your own), water purification tablets, fork and spoon
- Twine, toilet paper, paper and pencil, safety pins, hand soap and dish soap, matches, a candle
- Flashlight with good batteries (keep batteries separately wrapped and replace annually)
- Combination maintenance tool (screwdrivers, pliers, knife, etc.)
- Medical Power of Attorney for each non-minor family member

- For security reasons, do not keep copies of social security numbers, birth certificates, blank checks or other sensitive items in your car.
- Keep in purse or wallet: credit card, driver's license, and extra cash.
- Keep "important papers" in fireproof box at home:
- Photocopies of credit card, driver's license and other documents from wallet or purse (for replacement purposes)
- Social security cards, birth certificates, immunization records, fingerprints and photos of family members
- Deed/titles of home and cars
- Insurance policies

Positive Attitude

Have a positive attitude no matter what happens. Look at the glass as half-full, not half-empty, referring to the success of your trip. With preparation for the basics, you can treat problems as adventures, not as trials. While waiting for car repairs, explore a business in the area, sing your family song, or complete a crossword puzzle. A positive attitude is especially important for the children, who can become frightened if their parents seem lost or fearful. When things go wrong, as they sometimes will, stay calm and think through your options.

Teamwork

Choose the travel plan that works well for all of your family and include everyone in the planning. Some parents like to be spontaneous with their vacation. While last-minute decisions may be creative for the person planning it, they are often very disruptive to the rest of the family and rob others of the chance to plan ahead and contribute. Remember that you are part of a team and that others have plans, projects and on-going interests different from yours. A good friend of ours tells her kids the date and duration of surprise trips, but not the destination. That way she preserves the spontaneity, but avoids conflicts. An open family discussion may help you find the right approach for your group.

Chapter 8
Enjoying Hiking and Camping

The best things in life are not things.
—Author Unknown

A Wonderful Gift

The greatest gift we received at my husband's college graduation was a used eight foot by eight foot tent that his parents gave to us. I had not grown up in a camping family but I was quickly converted. My husband's first job after college was in New England. Anxious to use our "new" tent, we jumped at the chance to travel to Vermont to attend an office campout and enjoy the gorgeous autumn colors. In spite of the cold temperatures, we pitched the tent close to a nearby cabin and plugged in an electric blanket to keep us warm. It was our one-year-old daughter's first camping trip. Others had nicer equipment, but we were happy. We were made welcome and enjoyed getting acquainted with our new friends.

That weekend the Alldredge family camping memories began. Since then we have enjoyed the beauties of nature in many parts of the country. We have hiked wild trails, enjoyed quaking aspen rustling in the breeze, seen stars brighter than any near the city, observed deer, elk, turkeys, wild pigs, coyotes,

squirrels and other animals in the wild, watched fish jump in a lake, admired waterfalls—big and small—and shared songs and stories around glowing campfires. The family memories are sweet and lasting and we are pleased that our grown children are now enjoying the same adventures with their little ones.

Family camping is an inexpensive way to create wonderful memories, to encourage close family ties and to develop character. It is great to leave the neighborhood, the laundry, and the cleaning behind. We have found that—like magic—bickering and whining are also left behind. Kids learn to entertain themselves with the wonders of nature rather than with store-bought toys and high-tech programming.

Simplicity

Camping can be easy. At first, blankets and throw rugs can provide the needed bedding. In most areas a tent is essential to protect against nighttime insects and rain, and many stores sell tents for less than the cost of a one-night stay at a hotel. Other basic equipment includes a lantern, a large cast iron fry pan or griddle, a cooler for perishable foods, and a water jug. Other cooking and eating utensils may be brought from the kitchen. Sleeping bags are nice but can be added later. A propane stove is also helpful, but not required. Camp equipment makes excellent Christmas and birthday gifts, so there are plenty of opportunities to gradually add more comfort and convenience. As you might imagine, we have made sure that our kids received a tent as a wedding or Christmas gift.

The best tents have a waterproof floor, large windows with netting and window covers that fold back so you can enjoy the breeze on warm days. Most tents now have a netted opening in the top and a separate cover so condensation does not form on the interior of the tent at night.

Start with a one-night camp at a nearby location. Then if things do not work out, you can always run home for an important item that you have forgotten. Keep a positive attitude and enjoy the outdoors and the challenge. Enjoy the smells of a campfire or of a mossy spring, the sound of the wind in the trees, the sight of bats and birds catching insects in the air—all these are free and come to you just by being there and noticing them. Soon your kids will be collecting insects, plants, and colorful rocks and you will all be studying the star constellations.

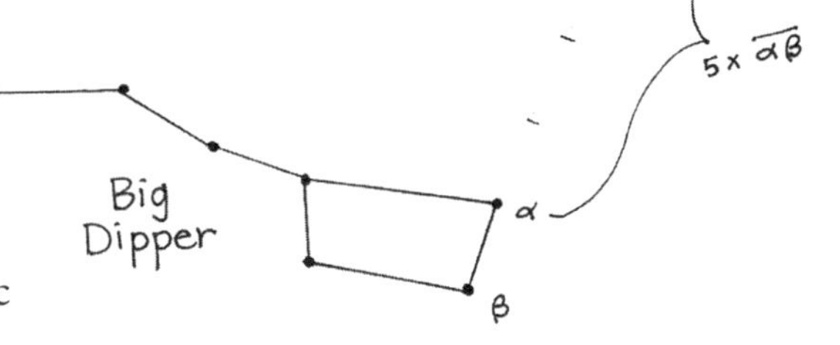

Every area has some public land on which camping is allowed, whether in large national forests or in smaller state parks. In areas with little public forest, consult AAA, the internet, or your local library for private campgrounds.

Compact Schedules and Fun Food

We all lead busy lives. In order to find time for camping, we often left after work on Friday evening and drove to a favorite spot just thirty minutes away. With a little practice, setting up the tent, laying out the bedrolls, and starting the fire only took a short while, even after dark. After roasting hot dogs and marshmallows, we enjoyed the fire for a while, sang songs, told stories, and went to bed. With the coming of morning we cooked a good breakfast of bacon and pancakes while the kids played catch with Frisbees or explored the area.

To us, breakfast has always tasted better cooked out-of-doors—perhaps it's just the novelty. After breakfast, we usually cleaned up and hiked for an hour or so.

We often chose camping spots near water. Many pleasant hours were filled with rock-hopping and catching pollywogs, frogs, crawdads and occasionally a fish. After a morning of exploring we fixed lunch—normally hamburgers with a piece of fruit—then cleaned up and drove home. In less than twenty-four hours, we had created memories that would last a lifetime. We still had time for those pesky weekend chores, for church, and for socializing with friends. Any inconvenience was well worth it.

I frequently had a baby or toddler to tend. The babies seemed to enjoy being in a front pack and I could better monitor their condition there. The toddlers preferred a backpack and sometimes I would carry one child while my husband carried another. Many stores have the backpack child carriers, but you may have to search a bit for the front packs.

My husband always enjoyed cooking over an open fire and, if you know how, this is the least expensive and most fun way to cook in camp. Dian Thomas' bestselling book, *Roughing It Easy,* is an excellent reference on basic camp cooking. Some campgrounds require you to bring your own wood or prohibit open fires so before you go, call the Forest Service or the campground host to be sure open fires are allowed. Propane stoves are inexpensive and easy to use, but, where possible, a small fire adds a great deal to the atmosphere of a camp. Of course cooking is not absolutely necessary. You can have cold cereal or bagels for breakfast and make sandwiches for lunch. When hiking, a granola bar and a piece of fruit make a quick and easy meal.

Tin foil dinners are inexpensive, easy to prepare, fun to cook and eat, and quick to clean up—ideal for quick camping trips.

Tin Foil Dinners

1½ lbs ground beef

½ cabbage

4 to 6 carrots

1 to 2 onions

3 large (or six small) potatoes

Salt and pepper

Aluminum foil

1. Tear aluminum foil into 12 rectangles, each 18 inches long.
2. Form ground beef into ½ lb. patties and place in the center of the foil rectangles.
3. Cut the cabbage into wedges, separate the leaves and place under and over the ground beef patties.
4. Slice the carrots, potatoes and onions and place on the cabbage.
5. Salt and pepper to taste.
6. Fold the aluminum foil around the food, rolling the edge to form a seal. Fold a second foil rectangle around the first, placing the seal on the opposite side as the first.
7. Place on hot coals for 20 to 35 minutes (less time for very hot coals or fire, more time for cooler coals), turning every few minutes with a stick, glove or pliers. You can usually hear the fat from the meat sizzling. When the food seems cooked, pull a dinner out of the fire, open it and check to see if it is done.
8. Adjust the ingredients to your taste. Chicken can be used instead of hamburger and bell peppers can be added if you prefer.
9. Makes six dinners.

When camping near the car, you can cook nearly everything available at home if you take the necessary pots and pans, keep the food in a cooler and learn to use a dutch oven.

A dutch oven is a heavy cast iron pot that is put directly on the fire and can be used as an oven or a pot. When away from the car, you might try some of the following suggestions.

Breakfast

- Bagels and cream cheese (use squeeze-type packages)
- Oatmeal or cracked wheat cereal (requires small aluminum pot, water, and a fire or portable stove) eaten dry or with powdered milk or packaged milk that requires no refrigeration
- Fruit (dried or fresh)

Lunch

- Dry soup mix (requires small aluminum pot, water, and a fire or portable stove)
- Freeze-dried foods of many kinds (require small aluminum pot, water, and a fire or portable stove)
- Peanut butter and jelly sandwiches (these travel well in a backpack)
- Granola bars, jerky or trail mix
- Fruit (dried or fresh)

Dinner

- Biscuits and gravy (make a stiff dough from pre-mixed biscuits, spread half inch deep dough on greased foil, wrap and bake on cool coals, or wrap on a stick and roast over coals like a hot dog or marshmallow; mix gravy in a small pan from a packaged mix)
- Baked potato (wrap in foil and bake in the coals of the campfire, add catsup, butter or seasonings from small packages that require no refrigeration)
- Baked beans or canned vegetables (heated on the fire in the original can—be sure to open the can before placing on the fire)
- Freeze-dried meals of many kinds (requires a small aluminum pot, water, and a fire or portable stove)

In many areas, squirrels and other wild animals raid food containers during the night. To prevent this, put food in the trunk of the car or in a trash bag hanging on a string a foot below a tree limb.

Make a convenient hand-washing station by poking a small hole in the lower side of an empty Clorox jug and plugging the hole with a golf tee. When in camp, fill the jug with water and hang it on a nearby tree. When the lid of the jug is loosened and the tee is removed, a thin stream of water is emitted. A bar of soap in the toe of an old nylon knee-high stocking can be hung on the handle of the jug, providing handy access. Just rub your wet hands on the outside of the stocking and the soap will come through.

Each time we left a campground, regardless of how we found it, we and the kids picked up any trash we could find. It seemed somehow easier to do if we asked each one to find twenty pieces of litter before we left. This taught the kids to be tidy and to respect others. Another small way we taught this lesson was to have a child retrieve anything they threw from the van. While traveling, if one of the kids threw wastepaper out the window, my husband would stop the van, back up, and have the offender pick up the litter.

Hot Dog/Marshmallow Roasting Sticks

Everyone needs a set of hot dog/marshmallow roasting sticks. These also make great gifts.

Hot Dog/Marshmallow Roasting Sticks

Materials:

48 inches of 3/4 inch diameter wooden dowel

Eight stainless steel welding rods, each 36 inches long, 1/8"
    diameter (copper rods are too flexible)

Elmer's glue

Polyurethane protective coating (optional)

One used, slim denim pant leg (24"
    long) and one shoe lace (optional)

Tools:

Wood saw

Drill and 1/8" bit

Step One

Cut the dowel into 6 inch lengths.

Step Two

Use a 1/8" drill bit to drill a hole,
    as straight as possible, into one
    end of each dowel piece and
    about 1½" deep.

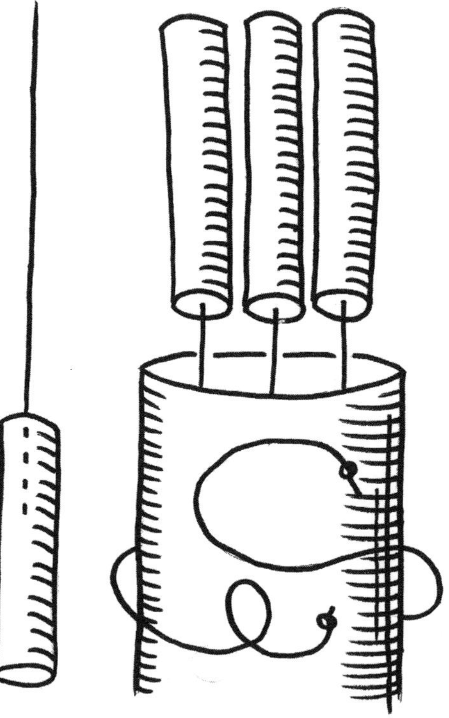

Step Three

Squirt some glue into the hole and insert a welding rod. Hold the rod in the hole for about one minute or until the compressed air doesn't push it back out.

Step Four

Optional—Coat the dowels with polyurethane or paint (preserves the dowels).

Step Five

Optional—Make a bag to hold the roasting sticks. Sew closed (or tie with a shoe lace) one end of the pant leg. Slide the roasting sticks into the bag, so that the handles are outside the bag. Tie a shoe lace (or cord or rope) around the top of the bag.

Step Six

Optional—If you have more than one set of roasting sticks in the family, you can color-code them by painting the ends of the handles different colors. Makes eight sticks.

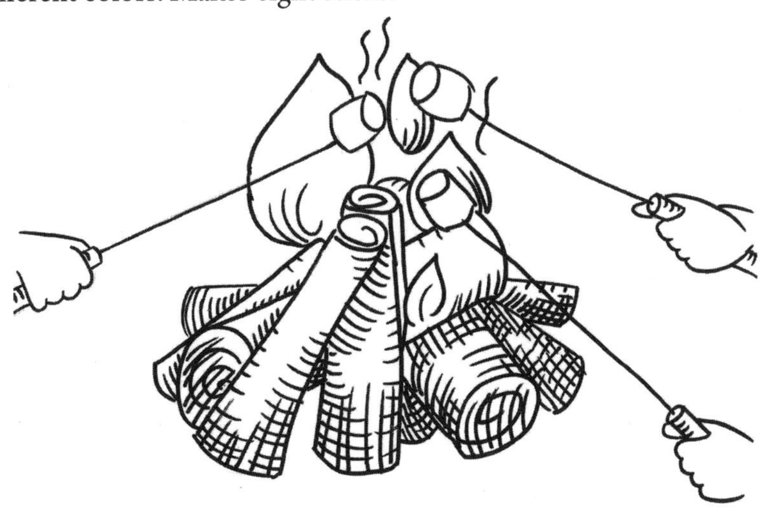

Safety Tips

Many campgrounds are located in fairly settled areas with few natural dangers. In other areas, campers should pay attention to warnings of such things as cliffs or fast-running rivers. In the wild, animals generally want to get away from you even more than you want to get away from them. They can be aggressive if you corner or attack them, so it is best to just let them go their way. If you have further questions regarding safety issues in your camping area, call the Forest Service Office, campground host or other local official. Common sense is the key to safety, whether in the wild or in the city.

Insects are not a problem in most areas of the U.S. but there are exceptions. If insects are troublesome in your area, consider choosing a time of the year when those pests are not yet out in force. Learn what repellents work well and use them as directed.

Most wild water sources are not suitable for drinking unless purified in some way. I suggest that you carry the water you need and keep a gallon or so in the car as backup. On longer hiking trips, water can be purified with tablets, with special filters, or by boiling vigorously for twenty minutes.

Before hiking, let those at camp know where you are going and when you will return. Take water, a map, a compass, and a small first aid kit.

A Final Pitch

I encourage you to try family camping in one form or another. Henry David Thoreau said, "To be admitted to Nature's hearth costs nothing. None is excluded, but excludes himself. You have only to push aside the curtain." Dealing with Nature builds character, self reliance, patience, and most of all appreciation for the basics. Boys and girls both learn to appreciate the unparalleled beauty of the earth—the flowers, trees, birds, and moving water, a developing sunset, the rising moon, and the busy sounds of birds, crickets and rustling leaves. An inner peace comes from escaping the hubbub of the city to a place where you can think deeply about life.

For many, it is worth a bit of dirt and inconvenience to have the adventure, the peace and the beauty. Humans are washable, after all. It is exhilarating to test our limits, to do something unusual, to be where others rarely go, and to see Nature wild and untouched.

When our youngest was about two years old, we convinced my family, who were not very big on camping, to backpack a mile and a half into Round Willow Bottom. This small lake lies in a spruce and aspen forest high in the Rocky Mountains. Forty of us, including our own eleven, carried tents, sleeping bags and enough food for three days to the edge of the lake. We cooked over the fire, swam in the icy water, and played "Run, Sheep, Run," a group game of "Hide and Seek". The women and younger children slept in tents while the men and older kids slept under the stars. Now, many years later, they all have fond memories of the lake in the morning, the grasshoppers and flowers in the meadow, the towering mountains and fresh fish frying on the fire.

A year or two after the Round Willow Bottom experience, our own family hiked a mile from the highway into the desert foothills a few miles from our home. As usual we left home after work on a Friday and, after cooking tin foil dinners near the car, we hiked up a familiar trail in the dark, using lanterns for light. We camped on a ridge and climbed into our sleeping bags (my husband and I carried extras for the smaller ones). In the morning we awoke to a great view of the valley, with cars on the highway far below and desert flowers on all the hills. Even today, we often reflect on the beauty of that view.

I cannot relate here all our many family camping experiences. During our children's formative years, we probably averaged five camps each year, sometimes in the desert and sometimes in the mountain pines. For us, camping and hiking created wonderful family memories and taught our kids valuable lessons.

If I cannot talk you into backpacking, take your kids and camp near your vehicle. Drive to a beautiful state park and pitch your tent near the car. Many families make wonderful memories cooking with a propane stove, sleeping on a cot in an established campground, and enjoying day hikes in the park. The cost is modest, the flowers are still colorful, the birds still sing, and your kids can learn many of the same lessons.

If it is not worth the inconvenience to you to camp, by all means take your family hiking and picnicking. Take pictures; build memories. Stay in a hotel if you must, but then walk along a stream, climb a hill, listen to the birds, study the flowers, look at the stars at night and teach your kids to recognize at least one constellation (the stars are much brighter away from the lights of the city). Please do not take the beauties of the earth for granted. Ralph Waldo Emerson put it this way, "If the stars should appear but one night every thousand years how man would marvel and stare."

Chapter 9
Believing in Your Family

The only time we fail in the home is when we give up on each other.
—Marvin J. Ashton

Whatever the size of your family and whether they are young or nearly grown, it is *your* family. Each child is your stewardship to love, to teach and to protect. Nurturing a family is not always easy or fun, but remember that you are building human lives, lives that will affect many others. These times together with your kids do make a difference. The kids will remember them all of their lives—the smiles, the working, the learning, the exploring, and the overcoming. In later challenging times these memories will give them courage instead of discouragement and confidence instead of fear.

As I look at our eleven grown kids, I am most grateful. Within the coming year, all will be college graduates and are responsible individuals. They love music and play musical instruments. All are great cooks, including the boys. Eight are happily married and are enjoying family life with their kids. The other three are progressing in the same direction. It pleases me that those who have their own families are now setting Summer Goals with their kids. The memories of their youth are pleasant enough and the effort rewarding enough for them to want their kids to experience the same.

One of our daughters, the mother of her own five children, says, "My kids *love* Summer Goals. They look forward to them. To the children, Summer Goals are not chores—they are a list of fun things to do. We have accomplished so much more during the summer because of them."

These activities are easy to enjoy. Remember to modify them according to your family size and the ages of your kids. The important part is to enjoy them, to plan ahead a bit and to follow through on your plan.

My husband and I have been blessed by a caring God with healthy, responsive children and we readily acknowledge that their success is due to more than our actions alone. However, we also believe that part of the credit belongs to the activities outlined in this book and to the fun and learning we accomplished together during school vacations.

Each of you has also been blessed with wonderful, capable children. You only have to believe in them and in yourself and to explore their capabilities. I am confident that you and they will be happier as a result. You can do it! Believe in yourself and in your family!

Twelve Things To Remember

The value of time.
The value of perseverance.
The pleasure of working.
The dignity of simplicity.
The worth of character.
The power of kindness.
The obligation of duty.
The virtue of patience.
The wisdom of economy.
The improvement of talent.
The joy of originating.
The influence of example.

—Author Unknown

Additional Resources

Family Resources and Child Development

Getting Unplugged: Take Control of Your Family's Television, Video Game, and Computer Habits, Joan Anderson and Robin Wilkins, John Wiley & Sons, 1998

Recipe Makeovers—Homemade for Health—Cooking for Lower Cancer Risk, American Institute for Cancer Research, 1759 R Street NW, Washington, DC 20090-7167, copyright 2005, www.aicr.org

Strengthening America's Families: Exemplary Parenting and Family Strategies for Delinquency Prevention, Karol, L. Kumpfer, U.S. Department of Justice, Office of Juvenile Justice and Delinquency Prevention, University of Utah, April 1999

What Kids Really Want That Money Can't Buy – Tips for Parenting in a Commercial World, Betsy Taylor, Warner Books, 2003

Summer Learning

Kids in the Kitchen—Recipes for Fun, Gooseberry Patch, 2006, Delaware, OH (recipes for children)

Summer Bridge Activities, by Rainbow Bridge Publishing (school exercises and activities—to continue school work, available for each school grade)

The Read-Aloud Handbook, by Jim Trelease, Penguin Books, 1982 (good ideas for reading to your kids)

Monthly Newsletter, The NYU Child Study Center, June 2006

Parent Letter, The NYU Child Study Center, June 2004

Pensacola News Journal, Kate Suchcicki, May 27, 2008

www.creativekidsathome.com (science projects for kids)

www.lancaster.unl.edu/food/foodsafety.shtml
   (home cooking safety recommendations)
www.summerreadingnys.org/parents
   (good reading suggestions)

Summer Activities

www.scouting.org (Boy Scouts of America – activities for boys)
www.girlscouts.org (Girls Scouts of America – activities for girls)
www.parents.com (activities and parenting advice)
www.lifescript.com (activities)
www.crochet.about.com (crocheting)
Play It Again, Kids, *Colorado Springs Gazette* and Freedom Colorado
   Information, Inc., reprinted in the *East Valley Tribune*, Phoenix, 2008 (jacks,
   marbles, hopscotch and jump rope)

Camping

www.nps.gov (National Park Service)
www.us-parks.com (National Park and camping information)
   (see state Web sites for state parks)

Appendix A

More Examples of Summer Goal Sheets

<table>
<tr><td colspan="3" align="center">Summer Goals for <u>Girl Age 12</u></td></tr>
<tr><td>How Many Times</td><td align="center">Item</td><td>Completed</td></tr>
<tr><td>4</td><td>Clean drawers (her own)</td><td></td></tr>
<tr><td>1</td><td>Clean drawers (family)</td><td></td></tr>
<tr><td>4</td><td>Wash and dry laundry</td><td></td></tr>
<tr><td>3</td><td>Clean windows</td><td></td></tr>
<tr><td>Help</td><td>Make a quilt</td><td></td></tr>
<tr><td>1 shorts</td><td>Sew article of clothing</td><td></td></tr>
<tr><td>3</td><td>Clean bathroom</td><td></td></tr>
<tr><td>1</td><td>Clean closet (her own)</td><td></td></tr>
<tr><td>1</td><td>Clean closet (family)</td><td></td></tr>
<tr><td>2</td><td>Clean cupboard</td><td></td></tr>
<tr><td>4</td><td>Vacuum the floor</td><td></td></tr>
<tr><td>2</td><td>Clean car</td><td></td></tr>
<tr><td>1</td><td>Bake cookies from scratch</td><td></td></tr>
<tr><td>1</td><td>Bake cake from scratch</td><td></td></tr>
<tr><td>1</td><td>Bake sweet rolls from scratch</td><td></td></tr>
<tr><td>Help</td><td>Bake dinner rolls from scratch</td><td></td></tr>
<tr><td>Help</td><td>Bake bread from scratch</td><td></td></tr>
<tr><td>2</td><td>Make dinner</td><td></td></tr>
<tr><td>2</td><td>Make breakfast</td><td></td></tr>
<tr><td>8 pages</td><td>Write in journal</td><td></td></tr>
<tr><td>2</td><td>Learn new piece on piano</td><td></td></tr>
<tr><td>1</td><td>Learn new vocal solo</td><td></td></tr>
<tr><td>4</td><td>Read books</td><td></td></tr>
<tr><td></td><td></td><td></td></tr>
</table>

Summer Goals for <u>Girl Age 7</u>

How Many Times	Item	Completed
1	Clean drawers (her own)	
1	Clean drawers (family)	
1	Wash and dry laundry	
2	Clean windows	
	Make a quilt	
	Sew article of clothing	
2	Clean bathroom	
1	Clean closet (her own)	
2	Clean closet (family)	
2	Clean cupboard	
2	Vacuum the floor	
1	Clean car	
Help	Bake cookies from scratch	
Help	Bake cake from scratch	
Help	Bake sweet rolls from scratch	
Help	Bake dinner rolls from scratch	
Help	Bake bread from scratch	
Help	Make dinner	
1	Make breakfast	
5 pages	Write in journal	
5	Learn new piece on piano	
2	Learn new vocal solo	
50	Read books	
1	Memorize word flash card sets	
1 each	Memorize addition and subtraction card sets	

Summer Goals for <u>Grandson Age 5</u>

Item	Completed
Read books with Mom or Dad	
Learn to write your name	
Learn to recognize all the letters of the alphabet	
Learn to sing a song	
Memorize one verse of the Holy Bible	
Write letters to cousins or friends	
Help make dinner	
Help make bread	
Help make cookies	
Help clean the bathroom	
Help wash loads of laundry	
Help dry loads of laundry	
Help sort socks	
Help take out the trash	
Help sew a marble bag	
Plant something in the garden	
Help weed the garden	
Help harvest the garden	
Learn to do a back bend	
Learn to swim without floaties	
Help plan and carry out a service project	
Practice the piano for ten minutes each	
Unload the dishwasher	
Load the dishwasher	
Learn to tie your shoes	
(Note: Daughter's format)	

Summer Goals for __Granddaughter Age 3__

Item	Completed
Help make a quilt	
Weed in the garden	
Harvest in the garden	
Memorize a verse of the Holy Bible	
Learn one song to sing	
Learn to do a somersault	
Help clean the bathroom	
Help clean one closet	
Help clean windows	
Help load the dishwasher	
Help unload the dishwasher	
Help make dinner	
Help do two loads of laundry - wash	
Help do two loads of laundry - dry	
Help dust a room	
Help make cookies	
Help make bread	
Help sew an article of clothing	
Help plan and carry out a service project	
Write two letters	
Help write two emails	
Read ten books with Mom or Dad	
(Note: Daughter's format)	

Summer Goals for _______________________		
How Many Times	**Item**	**Completed**

Appendix B

Play Scripts

There is no comparison between that which is lost by not succeeding
and that which is lost by not trying.
—Francis Bacon

- These plays are meant to be enjoyable.

- Remember, there is no right or wrong.

- Adjust the dialogue for the ages of your kids, or just make it up as you go.

- Arrange to perform for a small audience such as a family group or an invited group of neighbors. Having a set date to work toward makes it more special for the kids.

- You can do it!

The Three Little Pigs

The play begins with the three little pigs talking with their Mother pig and saying:

1st Little Pig: "Mother, we are going out into the world to seek our fortune."

2nd Little Pig: "Yes, we want to go."

Mother pig: "There is a big bad wolf out there in the woods and he likes to eat little pigs! Please be careful."

3rd Little Pig: "Don't worry Mom, we will be just fine."

And the three little pigs run off together skipping and singing: "Who's afraid of the big bad wolf, the big bad wolf, the big bad wolf; who's afraid of the big bad wolf, Tra la la la la.

Soon they come to a man selling straw. (He could be a fictional person or a real person depending on how many you need to involve)

1st Little Pig: "Sir, I want to hurry and build a house out of straw. I want to go play. May I buy that straw?"

1st Man: "Of course you may buy my straw." The 1st little pig pulls pretend coins or paper coins from his pocket and hands them to the 1st man.

While the 1st little pig is busily building his house of straw (the cardboard straw house is laying on the floor so that the little pig can pretend to be building his house, with big motions he builds his house and then picks up the cardboard house and hides behind it holding it up with both hands.

The other two little pigs hurry off to find the materials to build their houses. They come to a second man with a load of sticks and the 2nd little pig decides he would like to build his house with sticks.

2nd Little Pig: "Sir, I want to build a nice house out of sticks. May I buy those sticks from you?"

2nd Man: "Yes, I will sell these sticks to you for your house." The second little pig pulls several coins from his pocket and hands them to the man. He then pretends to build his house as he stands by the stick cardboard house. He takes a little longer than the 1st little pig to build his house, but then picks up his cardboard house and hides behind it.

Now the 3rd little pig hurries on his way and says: "I want a really, really strong house. I may have to work harder and longer, but I don't want the big bad wolf to eat me!"

The 3rd little pig skips in circles around the other little pigs, but before long he comes to a man selling a pile of imaginary bricks and asks: "Sir, I have been working and saving to buy bricks because I want to build a very strong house so the big bad wolf won't eat me. Will you sell your bricks to me?"

3rd Man: "I will be glad to sell my bricks to you." The little pig pulls coins from both pockets to pay the man for the bricks. This all takes place over the cardboard brick house that has been lying on the floor, and the little pig pretends to very carefully build his house of bricks. He then picks up the cardboard brick house and hides behind it.

After a little time has passed, the big bad wolf makes his appearance by striding onto the scene. He rubs his tummy and says: "I am very hungry. I think a little pig would taste very good right now."

The wolf looks around and spies the little house of straw and walks up to the door, knocks, and growls: "Little pig, little pig, let me come in!"

1st Little Pig (in a meek and scared voice): "Not by the hair of my chinny, chin, chin, will I open my door so that you can come in."

Wolf (growling): "Then I'll huff and I'll puff and I'll blow your house in!" The wolf begins to huff and puff. He only has to huff and puff a few times until he blows the house down and the 1st little pig drops the cardboard house,

SCREAMS, and runs to the 2nd little pig's house of sticks, with the wolf hot on his trail. He barely makes it to the house of sticks and hides behind it with the 2nd little pig when the upset wolf knocks loudly on the door.

Wolf (growling very loudly): "Little pigs, little pigs, let me come in!"

2nd Little Pig (with a little confidence): "Not by the hair of my chinny, chin, chin, will I open my door so that you can come in."

Wolf (roaring): "Then I'll huff and I'll puff and I'll blow your house in!" The wolf begins to huff and puff. He huffs and puffs and huffs and puffs 3 or 4 times before the little cardboard house of sticks falls to the ground. The 2 little pigs SCREAM and run as fast as they can go, with the wolf trying hard to catch them. They get to the 3rd little pig's house of bricks just in time to hide before the wolf catches them.

By now the wolf is very angry and very hungry and says: "I want little pigs to eat, and I am very angry!" He then pounds on the door of the little brick house and roars: "Little pigs, little pigs, let me come in!"

3rd Little Pig (with great confidence): "Not by the hair of my chinny, chin chin, will I open the door so that you can come in." The wolf begins to huff and puff, huff and puff, and huff and puff some more, but he cannot blow the house down. He is very angry and determined to get those little pigs so he attempts to go down the chimney. He slips around the side of the little brick house but the little pigs have a pot of boiling water waiting for the wolf and he falls behind the big black pot. The little pigs can drop the house but hold the pot with the wolf in a heap behind it.

The three little pigs then take hands and dance around the wolf singing: "Who's afraid of the big bad wolf, the big bad wolf, the big bad wolf? Who's afraid of the big bad wolf, tra, la, la, la, la."

THE END

Scenery and Costumes for The Three Little Pigs

- Obtain a stove or refrigerator box from an appliance store and, with a serrated knife, cut the box into four pieces by cutting the corners of the box. If waste cardboard is not available, use poster board.

- Draw pictures of a straw house, a stick house, and a brick house on each of three pieces of cardboard. Tempera paint works well for color.

- On the fourth piece of cardboard, draw a big black pot and cut it out.

- Cut brown construction paper for the ears, nose, and tail of the wolf.

- Cut pink construction paper for the ears, nose, and tail of the mother and three pigs.

- Use hair pins or tape to attach the construction paper.

- You may add whatever other props you like. Scenery can be as simple or as complex as you wish.

- Use your imagination.

- Have fun!

The Little Red Hen and the Wheat

The play begins with the little red hen and her two or three fluffy chicks scratching in the yard with a dog, a cat and a pig lazily looking on.

Little Red Hen: "Look! Look! See what I have found. Who will help me plant these grains of wheat?"

Dog: "Not I. I have some very important bones to look after."

Cat: "Not I, for I have visitors coming in a few minutes."

Pig: "Not I. I don't know how to do things like that."

Little Red Hen: "Then I'll do it." She and her chicks pretend to plant the wheat.

The dog, the cat, and the pig only watch, and act bored, lazy, and disinterested after each request.

Little Red Hen: "Now, who will water the wheat?"

Dog: "Not I. I have other things to do today."

Cat: "Not I. I have to take a little nap in the sun."

Pig: "Not I. I must go and cool off in the shade."

Little Red Hen: "Then I'll do it." She and her chicks pretend to water the wheat.

Little Red Hen: "Now, who is going to weed this wheat?"

Dog: "Not I. That kind of work doesn't agree with me."

Cat: "Not I. I would not be able to tell the weeds from the wheat."

Pig: "Not I. I have so many other things to do."

Little Red Hen: "Then I'll do it." She and her chicks pretend to weed the wheat.

Dog: "What fine wheat we have."

Cat: "What fine wheat we have."

Pig: "What fine wheat we have."

Little Red Hen: "Yes, indeed, it is time to harvest the wheat. Who would like to harvest the wheat for us?"

Dog: "Not I."

Cat: "Not I."

Pig: "Not I."

Little Red Hen: "Then I'll do it." She pretends to carefully cut off each precious head of wheat and put it in a bag held open by the three chicks.

The little red hen calls to the dog, the cat, and the pig: Who will take this wheat to the mill to be ground into flour?"

Dog: "Not I. The dust would get into my nose and make me sneeze."

Cat: "Not I. You know I cannot carry such a heavy load."

Pig: "Not I. Why, I do not even know where the mill is."

Little Red Hen: "Well then, I'll do it." Along with her little chicks she pretends to carry it to the mill. She then brings the pretend sack of flour back and the dog, the cat, and the pig come to see the fine flour.

Little Red Hen: "Now, who is going to make this flour into bread?"

Dog: "Not I. I don't know how to make bread."

Cat: "Not I. I can't make bread either."

Pig: "Not I. I never made a loaf of bread in my life."

Little Red Hen: "Then I'll do it." She pretends to make the bread.

Little Red Hen: "Who will help me gather wood to build a fire?"

Dog: "Not I."

Cat: "Not I."

Pig: "Not I."

Little Red Hen: "Then I'll do it." She and her chicks pretend to gather wood.

Little Red Hen: "Now who is going to bake this bread?"

Dog: "Not I."

Cat: "Not I."

Pig: "Not I."

Little Red Hen: "Then I'll do it." She pretends to put it in the oven.

As the little red hen takes the loaf of bread from the oven she says: "Now who is going to eat this bread?"

Dog (very excitedly): "I will."

Cat (very excitedly): "I will."

Pig (very excitedly): "I will."

Little red hen: "Oh, no, you won't. My little chicks and I are going to eat it."

The little red hen and her chicks pretend to eat up the loaf of bread with the dog, the cat, and the pig sadly looking on.

THE END

Scenery and Costumes for The Little Red Hen

- Use colored construction paper to make ears, nose, and tails for each of the animals and attach with hair pins or tape.

- You may want to use a real loaf of bread for the finished product.

- You may want to use a real bow tie for the dog, a necklace for the cat, a hat for the pig, and an apron for the little red hen. Use your imagination.

- You may use whatever additional props you wish. Scenery and props can be very basic and still be great.

- Use your imagination.

- Have fun!

Goldilocks and the Three Bears

The play starts with the Three Bears sitting at a table with three bowls of porridge.

Father Bear tastes his porridge and exclaims: "Oh, this porridge is much too hot!"
Mother Bear: "Let's take a little walk in the woods while our porridge cools."
Baby Bear: "I like that idea."
The three bears exit laughing and singing.
A little girl comes skipping along and sees a little house. (The house could be pretended or you could make a little house, including a door, from a waste refrigerator box obtained from an appliance store. Tempera paint works well for painting scenery on cardboard.)
Goldilocks knocks at the door then knocks again. Finding no one home, she calls out: "Anybody home?" When there is no response, she opens the door and walks in.
Seeing the bowls of porridge on the table she remembers how hungry she is and says:
"I am so hungry, and this porridge looks delicious. I think I'll try some."
She tastes the big bowl of porridge, and finding it very hot, says: "Oh my, this is too hot."
She tastes the middle-sized bowl of porridge and says: "This is too cold."
She tastes the little bowl of porridge and feeling very satisfied, says: "This is just right." And she eats it all.
She rubs her tummy and smacks her lips, gets up, and moves to the next area where there are large, medium, and small chairs. The medium chair should have a cushion or pillow on it. (Of course, you can pretend that they are there, but it is more fun to have real chairs.)
Goldilocks sits on the big hard chair and says: "This chair is too hard."
She sits on the medium chair and says: "This chair is much too soft."

She sits on the little chair and says: "This chair is just right." Suddenly she falls to the floor (pretending that it broke).

She acts sad and says: "Oh Dear."

Goldilocks moves to another area where there are three blankets folded on the floor, a larger one for Father Bear with no pillow, a medium blanket for Mother Bear covered with cushions, and a smaller blanket for the Baby Bear with one small pillow.

She yawns and says: "I feel so sleepy. Here is a nice bed to lie on."

She lies on the big bed and says: "This bed is much too hard."

She lies on the medium bed and says: "This bed is much too soft."

She lies on the baby bear's bed and quickly falls fast asleep.

Shortly, the three bears come home.

Mother bear: "What a nice walk."

Father bear: "Let's eat."

Baby bear: "I'm so hungry." They all sit down at the table to eat their porridge.

Father bear looks at his porridge and roars: "Someone has been eating my porridge."

Mother bear looks at her porridge and says sweetly: "Someone has been eating my porridge."

Baby bear (in a squeaky little voice): "Someone has eaten all my porridge!"

They move to the chairs.

Father bear sits on his chair and booms: "Oh my, someone has been sitting on my chair."

Mother bear sits on her chair and says timidly: "Oh dear, someone has been sitting on my chair."

Baby bear looks at his chair and sadly says: "Someone sat on my chair and has broken it to pieces." He begins to cry.

They move to the beds.

Father bear looks at his bed and growls: "Someone has been lying on my bed."

Mother bear looks at her bed and says patiently: "Someone has been lying on my bed."

Baby bear looks at his bed and cries: Oh my goodness, someone IS lying on my bed."

Goldilocks wakes up, sees the three bears, and runs away as fast as she can!

THE END

Scenery and Costumes for Goldilocks and the Three Bears

- Optional: Obtain a refrigerator box from an appliance store to use for the house. With a serrated knife cut away one side, leaving three sides. A refrigerator box is usually tall enough to allow you to make a door that a child can actually pass through. The kids may have to bend down a little to go through the door, but that is okay. Pretending that there is a house is okay too, depending on your available time and energy. Color your house with tempera paints.

- From construction paper, make ears, nose, and tails for the three bears. Use hair pins or tape to attach in the right places. Mother Bear could be wearing an apron.

- Goldilocks is a naïve little girl who might be wearing a dress and perhaps have a bow in her hair. If you prefer, a pair of jeans is fine.

- Locate large, medium, and small bowls. These could be from a set of mixing bowls from your kitchen cupboard.

- Locate three sizes of chairs.

- Get three blankets and a few pillows to make the beds.

- Use your imagination.

- Have fun!

Three Billy Goats Gruff

The play starts with the three billy goats wandering around pretending to eat grass.

Narrator: "There was a Little Billy Goat, a Middle-Sized Billy Goat, and a Big Billy Goat who lived on a mountain. They often looked down on the meadow below where the grass looked lush and green. They wanted very much to go to the meadow to eat the grass, but a river divided the mountain from the meadow. Just one bridge crossed over the river and a mean old troll lived under the bridge. He did not want anyone to cross over "his" bridge."

Little Billy Goat (in a squeaky little voice): "Look at that delicious grass in the meadow on the other side of the river."

Middle-Sized Billy Goat: "Let's cross the bridge and eat our lunch over there."

Big Billy Goat (in a big voice): "Oh my, there's an old troll under the bridge. He is very mean and likes to eat little goats."

Little Billy Goat: "I am little, and I am sure he won't want to eat me."

Middle-Sized Billy Goat: "You are so brave."

Big Billy Goat: "We will cross after you."

Little Billy Goat walks to the bridge and begins to cross a pretend bridge or one made out of cardboard. A person in the background hits two pieces of wood together to make a timid clip clopping sound as Little Billy Goat goes over the bridge.

As Little Billy Goat goes clip-clop, clip-clop, clip-clop over the bridge a loud growl is heard from the bridge where the old troll has been hiding: "Who is walking over my bridge?"

Little Billy Goat: "It is I, Little Billy Goat Gruff."

Troll (in a loud, roaring voice): "Stay right there, I am coming up to eat you!"

Little Billy Goat: "Please don't eat me. My bigger brother is coming along pretty soon and he is much fatter and juicier than I am."

Troll: "Okay, go ahead."

Little Billy Goat continues across the bridge with a person in the background hitting the wood together to make a clip clopping sound.

Middle-Sized Billy Goat now goes to the bridge and begins to go across. Someone in the background hits two pieces of wood together to make a louder clip-clopping sound as Middle-Sized Billy Goat goes over the bridge. As Middle-Sized Billy Goat goes clip-clop, clip-clop, clip-clop over the bridge a loud roar is heard from the bridge where the old troll has been hiding: "Who is walking over my bridge?"

Middle-Sized Billy Goat: "It is I, Middle-Sized Billy Goat Gruff. Please, don't eat me. My big brother is coming along pretty soon, and he is much, much fatter and juicier than I am."

Troll: "Okay, go ahead."

Middle-Sized Billy Goat continues across the bridge with someone in the background hitting the wood together to make a clip-clopping sound.

The two billy goats are happily eating grass in the meadow when Big Billy Goat approaches the bridge and begins to cross. A person in the background hits two pieces of wood together to make a very loud clip-clopping sound as Big Billy Goat goes over the bridge.

As Big Billy Goat confidently goes clip-clop, clip-clop, clip-clop over the bridge, a very loud roar is heard from the bridge where the old troll has been hiding: "Who is walking over my bridge?"

Big Billy Goat (confidently): "It is I, Billy Goat Gruff."

Troll: "Stay right there, I am coming up to eat you!"

Big Billy Goat (in his biggest voice): "Come right ahead."

The mean old troll comes on to the bridge and starts walking towards Big Billy Goat, but Big Billy Goat only tilts his head towards the mean old troll and walks toward him. The designated person hits pieces of wood together to make the loud clip-clopping sound of Big Billy Goat on the bridge. Big Billy Goat and the troll run together, and with his head Big Billy Goat butts the mean old troll off the bridge into the river. Big Billy Goat continues across the bridge as someone hits wood together for the clip-clopping noise.

Narrator: "The mean old troll turned into a rock at the bottom of the river and the three billy goats gruff were able to walk back and forth over the bridge to eat grass whenever they wanted."

THE END

Scenery and Costumes for Three Billy Goats Gruff

- Get a refrigerator or stove box from an appliance store.
- Cut down two corners where the seams are, making a smaller panel and a larger panel.
- Use one cardboard section to make a big rock for the troll to hide behind.
- Draw a bridge on the other three sections, laying them flat on the floor.
- Use gray or white construction paper to make ears, tail, and whiskers for the billy goats. You could make horns for the big billy goat gruff.
- Attach the construction paper with tape or hair pins, whichever works better.
- Use your imagination.
- Have fun!

Appendix C

Chime Music and Instructions

Making a Set of Hand-Held Pipe Chimes

Note: Only the "basic set" of chimes (those with color marks in the chart below) is required for the music we have provided. Lengths are very close to correct pitch. However, if it is important to you to obtain "perfect pitch," add 1/8" to the lengths in the chart, and then file down the end of each pipe until the pitch matches a tuning fork or a well-tuned piano.

Make twelve wooden mallets from materials purchased at a craft store. Cut 8" pieces from 3/8" diameter wooden dowels and glue into 1" round wooden heads (these usually come pre-drilled for 3/8" dowels).

Cut ½" diameter "thin-wall" electrical conduit to the lengths noted below. File off any sharp edges. Drill a 1/8" diameter hole all the way through each conduit piece (from one side to the other) about 1-1/2 inches from one end. Cut 10" lengths of heavy string, thread through the 1/8" holes, tie to form "handles", and cut off any excess string. With a black permanent marker, mark the note, the chord number and the chime number on each chime. Use colored markers or stickers to designate the colors on the chart (for easy identification by children).

(Optional) For carrying your chimes, make a 11" x 17" bag from jean fabric.

Chime #	Note	Length (Inches)	Color Marks	Chord #
1	B flat	13-3/8		
2	B	13	red, purple	V7, II
3	C (mid)	12-5/8	blue, yellow	IV, I
4	C sharp	12-1/4		
5	D	11-7/8	red, purple	V7, II
6	E flat	11-1/2		
7	E	11-1/4	yellow	I
8	F	10-7/8	blue, red	IV, V7
9	F sharp	10-11/16		
10	G	10-3/8	yellow, red, purple	I, V7, II
11	A flat	9-7/8		
12	A	9-9/16	blue	IV
13	B flat	9-3/8		
14	B	9-3/16	red, purple	V7, II
15	C (high)	8-7/8	blue, yellow	IV, I
16	C sharp	8-5/8		
17	D	8-5/16	red, purple	V7, II
18	E flat	8-1/8		
19	E	7-7/8	yellow	I

Most melodies have four basic chordal harmony accompaniments: I, IV, V7 and II. We have found that children recognize colors more easily than chord numbers and have substituted yellow (Y) for I, blue (B) for IV, red (R) for V7, and purple (P) for II. Chord numbers are often marked on popular music.

Rehearse the players briefly before they accompany the singing as follows:

1. Give each player one pipe and one mallet (eleven players). For smaller groups, use only the basic chimes numbers two through twelve (seven chimes). Four people can play this reduced basic set by holding two chimes in one hand and striking them both by wagging a mallet between them, moving the mallet rapidly from side to side so it strikes both chimes.

2. Show the players how to hold the pipe by its string handle, allowing it to hang freely.
3. Demonstrate striking the pipe crisply with the ball of the mallet right on the beat. (A) In 4/4 time strike on beats one and three. (B) In 2/4 time strike on both beats one and two. (C) In 3/4 time strike on beat one, maintaining a waltz-like tempo.
4. Instruct players to watch the chord chart closely as you point to each chord. (A) They should play only when you point to a chord with their color on it preparing in advance to strike in rhythm. (B) As director, you should prepare to move to the next chord slightly ahead of the beat so players can properly anticipate the beat. (C)Assume that the chord remains the same until a different chord is given.
5. Allow players to practice playing once or twice through the sequence of chords to be used in the song.
6. Handprint the songs with their chime cues on posterboard so the players can see them more easily.

You Are My Sunshine

(4/4 Time. Starting pitch is G, pipe 10.)

You are my sunshine, my only sunshine,
      Y   Y

You make me happy when skies are grey,
       B   Y

You'll never know dear how much I love you,
    B   Y

Please don't take my sunshine a-way.
     Y   R   Y

Twinkle, Twinkle, Little Star

(4/4 Time. Starting pitch C, pipe 3.)

Twinkle, twinkle, little star,
Y   Y   B   Y

How I wonder what you are.
R   Y   P   Y

Up a-bove the world so high,
Y   B   Y   P

Like a diamond in the sky.
Y   B   Y   P

Twinkle, twinkle, little star,
Y   Y   B   Y

How I wonder what you are.
R   Y   P   Y

Home On The Range

3/4 time, starting pitch is G, or pipe 10

Oh, give me a home where the buffalo roam,
   Y   Y   B   B

And the deer and the antelope play,
    Y   Y   P

Where seldom is heard a dis-couraging word
  Y   Y   B   B

And the skies are not cloudy all day.
    Y   R   Y

Home, home on the range
 Y   R   Y

Where the deer and the antelope play,
   Y   Y   P

Where seldom is heard a dis-couraging word,
  Y   Y   B   B

And the skies are not cloudy all day.
   Y   R   Y

Away in a Manger

3/4 time; starting pitch is G, or pipe 10

A-way in a manger, No crib for his bed,
  Y   Y   B   Y

The little Lord Jesus lay down his sweet head.
  P   R   Y   Y

The stars in the heaven looked down where he lay,
 Y   Y   B   Y

The little Lord Jesus a-sleep on the hay.
  R   Y   B   R Y

Be near me, Lord Jesus, I ask thee to stay,
  Y   Y   B   Y

Close by me for-ever, and love me, I pray.
  P   R   Y   Y

Bless all the dear children in thy tender care
 Y   Y   B   Y

And take us to heaven, to live with thee there.
  P   Y   B   R   Y

Jingle Bells

4/4 time, starting pitch is G or pipe 10

Dashing through the snow, in a one-horse open sleigh
Y   Y   Y   B

O'er the fields we go, laughing all the way;
B   R R   Y

Bells on bobtail ring, making spirits bright,
Y   Y   Y   B

What fun it is to ride and sing a sleighing song to-night.
B   P   R   Y

Jingle Bells, Jingle Bells, Jingle all the way;
Y   Y   Y   Y

Oh, what fun it is to ride in a one-horse, open sleigh;
B   Y   R   R

Jingle Bells, Jingle Bells, Jingle all the way;
Y   Y   Y   Y

Oh, what fun it is to ride in a one-horse, open sleigh.
B   Y   R   Y

Appendix D

More Games
Directions for Jacks, Marbles, Four Square,
Hopscotch and Jump Rope

Jacks

History

The first to play it, and we kid you not, were Cro-Magnon cave kids, who needed hand-eye coordination to become good hunters, according to the Strong National Museum of Play. Later on, the Egyptians played a similar game called knucklebones, using the toe bones from sheep. Over the centuries everything from stones to today's six-pronged metal jacks have been used.

Equipment

A small bouncy ball, 10 to 15 jacks. Sets can be bought at most variety stores for about $4 to $10 depending on how fancy they are. Some come with cloth bags to keep them in.

Players

Two to six is best if you don't want to sit there all day. And, of course, you can play against yourself if you want.

Who Goes First?

Each person throws all the jacks in the air, and the person who catches the most goes first.

Rules

The object is to pick up all the jacks. Scatter the jacks on a smooth, flat surface – the floor is best. Toss the ball up, pick up one jack, and after the ball has bounced once, catch it with the same hand. Then transfer the captured jack to the free hand. Continue picking up one at a time, until all jacks are picked up. Then throw the jacks again, and pick up two at a time until all are picked up. Then threes, fours, etc. In some sequences there will be leftover jacks. Pick them up as sets.

Mistakes that make you lose your turn: Using wrong hand to catch the ball; not picking up the correct number of jacks; allowing the ball or jack to touch your body while catching the ball; catching the ball with both hands; not holding the ball or jacks until task is complete; touching other jacks while trying to pick up a jack or group of jacks.

Too Cute

If you want to be considered an expert, call the rounds onesies, twosies, threesies, foursies, and so forth. If two jacks are touching, you can separate them. That's called "kissies."

Winner

The person who makes it first from onesies to tensies, and back down again to onesies (doesn't have to happen during one turn, so keep track of where you are in the sequence).

More Fun

There are a variety of ways to play, some depending on fancy ways to pick up the jacks and the ball.

If Bored

Quit the game and see how many jacks you can spin at a time. They look like little ballerinas.

Marbles

Think of marbles as billiards without the table. It's a game that rewards strategy, skill and being a hustler.

History

The game of marbles dates back to the ancient Egyptians who taught it to the Romans, who taught pretty much everyone else. Marbles became a popular game in the United States after 1902 when inexpensive machine-made glass marbles became available. A national championship tournament is held every year in Wildwood, New Jersey.

How to Play

Rules vary according to the region. One of the more popular games is called Ringer. Start by finding a hard, smooth surface (a sidewalk, a patch of dirt, mom's newly refinished floors) and drawing a circle. Tournament size is 10 feet, but if you're just starting out, try something smaller. Arrange 13 marbles in an X in the center of the circle. Then start the game by taking turns shooting at the marbles from the outside of the circle.

How to Shoot

Most marble sets come with several small marbles, called mibs, and a larger marble, called a taw or shooter. Hold the taw between your thumb and forefinger. Put your hand on the ground so that the knuckle of your forefinger touches the surface. Then flick the taw at the mibs with your thumb.

I Missed, So What?

If you shoot and miss, or hit the marbles but don't knock any out of the circle, your turn is over. The next person goes.

I Hit One!

If you knock at least one marble out of the circle but your taw rolls out, your turn is over, but you keep the marble you knocked out. If you knock one out and your taw is still in the circle, you get to keep the marble and go again, but you shoot from where the taw lies.

How Do I Win?

The first person to knock out seven marbles wins.

Four Square

The Basics

Few things are as satisfying as dropping a mighty "cherry bomb" on an unsuspecting victim. No, we're not talkin' explosives here, but the playground game four square. (A cherry bomb is schoolyard slang for spiking the ball.) Popular on playgrounds for decades, the game is sort of like tennis or volleyball without a net. Players stand in four separate squares (as the name implies) and hit a bouncy ball back and forth to each other until someone messes up. The game can be friendly and slow, or fast and competitive. Four square courts grace many playgrounds, and adult leagues are popping up around the country as "rejuveniles" embrace the nostalgia of the game and the lack of athleticism needed to have fun at it.

Equipment Needed

Rubber playground ball, chalk (or tape), flat space for court, four people.

Rules (Essentials)

The court is a large square (typically 16 feet on each side) subdivided into four sub-squares, numbered 1-4. Inside lines are out-of-bounds, while outside lines of the square are in. The player in Square 4 is king/queen/grand poopah. This player serves from the back corner of their square, bouncing the ball once and then hitting it nicely to another square; some leagues stipulate the serve goes diagonally to Square 1. The ball should bounce only once (or not at all) and then be hit into another square. Play continues until the ball bounces twice in a player's square, the ball is hit out-of-bounds, the ball is carried instead of struck, or otherwise isn't returned properly to another square. When that happens, the offending player is out. The player who is out leaves the court; remaining players rotate into any higher square that is vacated; and a new player enters in Square 1.

Rules (Custom)

The rules can vary playground to playground, so feel free to adapt as you go. Square 4 can call special rules before each serve. These rules can be ridiculous: Slap yourself on the forehead and say "boys have cooties" before each hit. Some common permutations are black jack (if you catch the ball before it bounces in your square, the player who hit it is out), underhand only (good for beginners and long volleys), or body language (use any part of your body).

Tips

Competitive play. For those who need to keep score . . . you score points based on the number of serves you can remain in Square 4.

Showdown

If two players can't resolve a dispute, they must have a showdown, a sudden-death round of two square with no custom rules. The winner stays in the game.

Hopscotch

History

Hopscotch, played by kids around the world, first was used to train warriors. Not such a sissy game after all, eh? Yet it's about as low-tech a game as you can get, requiring nothing more than chalk, a rock and a good sense of balance. You can play it just about anywhere that's flat, indoors or out. And variations on the rules have no limits.

What You Need

Something to draw the game board and a game piece. Indoors, use masking tape to create the board; outdoors, use a stick to draw in the dirt or chalk (a rock will do in a pinch) to draw on concrete or blacktop. For a game piece, or marker, use a rock, large button, bottle cap, or beanbag.

Playing Field

A standard hopscotch board has eight squares at least 16 inches square (smaller squares are difficult to land in; get too large and it'll be difficult to hop across). The first squares are laid out in a straight line, stacked one-two-three. Then, two squares sit side-by-side straddling the first three boxes. At this stage, your board will look like a large T. Next, draw one centered box and follow it with another double box. At the top of the board you can draw a rest space, or "home." Number the boxes 1-8.

Rules

Player One stands outside the first box and tosses his or her marker into Square 1. That player then hops over Square 1 to Square 2 on one foot, and then continues hopping to Square 8, touching one foot each in the side-by-side squares. At home, the player turns around and hops back, pausing in Square 2 to bend over and pick up his marker – without touching the ground and while balancing on one foot. Then the player hops in Square 1 and out of the board. Player One then continues his turn by tossing his marker into Square 2 and repeating the pattern. All hopping is done on one foot except for the side-by-side squares. A player must hop over any square where a marker has been placed. A player's turn ends if his marker fails to land in the proper square, he steps on a line, he puts a second hand or foot down, he hops into a square where a marker sits, or he puts two feet down in a single box. If a player is called out, he should place his marker in the square where he will resume playing on his next turn. Then it's the next player's turn.

Variations

There are plenty. One popular board is a spiral, with a path to the center marked as "squares." Rules are the same, but there are no side-by-side squares. You can draw a home square in the center or make players turn around without a rest. For more fun, add squares. Roman foot soldiers trained in full armor, carrying gear, on boards more than 100 feet long, according to streetplay.com. Training improved their agility for battle. It's believed children imitated the soldiers by drawing their own boards, and hopscotch spread across Europe. According to the Oxford English Dictionary, hopscotch is a compound of "hop" and "scotch," or scratched line.

Jump Rope

For generations young girls have enjoyed the pastime of jumping rope, taking over playgrounds with swinging ropes and nonsensical rhymes. Usually seen as a girly game, boys usually opt out of joining. But make no mistake, jumping rope ain't for pansies.

History

The Jump Rope Institute has traced skipping rope back to 17th century Egypt where locals perfected the sport of jumping over vines. Double Dutch, a game involving two ropes swinging simultaneously, has been traced to similar periods in the Middle

East and China, but became popular in urban neighborhoods of the United States in the 1970s. Still think it's a game for schoolgirls in saddle shoes? Try it.

How To

To jump rope alone, not much is needed. Just an eight-foot rope and the basic concept: hold one end of the rope in each hand, swing the rope over your head from back to front and jump. To jump rope with friends, you need at least three people and a rope that is at least 12 to 14 feet long. The two who will be turning the ropes will stand face-to-face about eight feet apart. The turners swing the rope in a large circle, the third person jumps in.

Double Dutch

To Double Dutch, you need at least three people, two ropes that are 12 to 14 feet long, and guts. Lots of guts. The basic concept is to turn the ropes in an egg-beater fashion – one will swing clockwise while the other swings counterclockwise, so when one is touching the ground, the other is directly above it in the air. The goal is to have the jumper leap into the ropes and continue jumping. It's all about timing – and having soft ropes. You will get hit at least a few times.

Sing Song

Rhymes often help jumpers perfect their timing. Double Dutch jumpers need a song with a quicker beat, so either speed up the song or check online for other rhymes. Here are a few classics to get you started:

> Hello operator, please give me number nine;
> And if you disconnect me, I'll paddle your ____.

> Flies are in the meadow, the bees are in the park;
> Miss Susie and her boyfriend are kissing in the
> D-A-R-K, D-A-R-K, D-A-R-K,
> Dark, dark, dark!

Cinderella, dressed in yella, went downstairs to kiss her fella.
She made a mistake, and kissed a snake.
How many doctors will it take? 1,2,3,4 . . .

Miss Mary Mack, Mack, Mack
All dressed in black, black , black
With silver buttons, buttons, buttons
All down her back, back, back
She asked her mother, mother, mother
For fifty cents, cents, cents
To see the elephant, elephant, elephant
Jump the fence, fence, fence
They jumped so high, high, high
They touched the sky, sky, sky
And didn't come back, back, back
Til the fourth of July, July, July

The preceding details were furnished by the Colorado Springs Gazette and Freedom Colorado Information, Inc.

About the Author

Lorraine J. Alldredge is the mother of eleven children and lives in Mesa, Arizona with Tony, her husband of forty-one years. Ten of her kids are college graduates and one is nearing graduation. All of them cook well and enjoy music, outdoor sports and family life.

Lorraine holds an Associate of Arts Degree in Family Living and is a past president of her local Parent Teachers Association. She was the 1984 Arizona State Young Mother representative for the American Mothers Association and has been, for most of her adult life, a leader of youth and women in her church and community.

Eight of Lorraine's eleven children are married and have children of their own—the cutest and smartest in the world, in her judgement. When she is not spending time with her children and grandchildren, she enjoys sewing, reading, baking, playing the piano, and hiking and camping with Tony.

Lorraine would love to hear of your experiences with the ideas in this book, whether successes or failures, as well as suggestions for entries in future editions. She is delighted to try to answer any questions. Email her at lorrall@ cox.net or visit her Web site at www.sowhatcankidsdo.com.